From Brokenness to Wholeness A 21-Day Journal:

The journey of hearing the voice of God.

Tawana Conner

From Brokenness to Wholeness A 21-Day Journal:

The journey of hearing the voice of God.

Tawana Conner

Gemlight Publishing LLC,
Gulfport, Mississippi

Dedication

I dedicate this book to my children La'Carmie (Lou), Candace, Craig Jr., Micah, and Kardell Eugene; my stepdaughter Trella Woodfork; and my grandchildren Kaci, Kayla, Lia, Taylor, Dillon, Kaleb, Derrian, Shawn, Caleb, Caden and Master.

May the love of God always be in your heart. Please know I love you, but God loves you more. If you don't know him, get to know him. We live in some perilous times, and we can't make it without him if you're looking for a friend, mother, father, sister, or brother. I'm a living witness that God has been the one who I could depend on.

When things seemed impossible, I looked to the Lord for strength; after all, he's the author and finisher of my faith, and he promised he would never leave me or forsake me.

If you don't know him, it's very simple to let him in your heart. Admit to God that you're a sinner, believe in Jesus Christ as your savior, confess your sins, ask him for forgiveness, and pray the sinner's prayer.

"Jesus, I know I'm a sinner and need your forgiveness. I believe only you can forgive sins. I ask you to come into my heart, forgive my sins, and be the ruler of my life. Thank you for saving me. In Jesus' name, amen."

Table of Contents

Acknowledgments and Thanks

First and foremost,

I thank God for his love, grace, and mercy upon my life. He has allowed me to give birth to a fresh journey and new beginnings. I give all of the glory and honor to God, Jehovah Jireh (my provider), who has been my shield and my exceedingly great reward.

To my spiritual parents Pastor Eunice and Apostle Eric Rush, thank you for your prayers and support while completely covering me. I thank God to have spiritual parents who walk in the anointing of God.

I thank God for the love and support from my husband Tommie, who has supported and loved me unconditionally, even through my brokenness. I praise God for you.

To my children and my parents, whom I love dearly, thanks for all of your love and support.

Note from the Author

Have you ever felt so broken like someone was stabbing your heart and shattering it into little pieces?

You may have also thought that nothing or no one could put the pieces back together? That's where I found myself four years ago. I thought I was broken beyond repair, but God guided me through a season of brokenness and purging. This season taught me God always has a plan, and he wanted to show me the fortitude I was capable of handling with his help.

Yes, it's true. We have seasons of brokenness, disappointments, rejections, and loneliness. Seasons represent a period of the year characterized by a fixed time and marked by a particular activity, event, or festivity.

1) Winter is associated with cold weather, holiday festivities, celebrations with loved ones, and feelings of jolliness. People during this season may also feel cold with an icy heart. They may have lost a loved one, struggled with a season of depression, or have a desire for friendly embraces and love.

2) Spring is associated with budding trees, blooming flowers, calming rain showers, and spring cleaning. Spring can be a refreshing time for people who want to make changes, start something new, throw out unnecessary clutter, or get organized. Spring may also be a season for crying.

3) Summer is associated with heat. Summer can be a time of intense passion or a time of unbearable pressure and stress.
4) Fall is associated with the gorgeous reds, oranges, and yellows of leaves changing color and the onset of cozy cool weather. Fall can be a romantic season, but it could also represent a time when people walk out of your life, leaving you with no one to support you.

God determines when our seasons start and end. The key to God releasing us from that season depends on our obedience. You have to listen to the voice of God and do what he tells you to do. If not, you'll end up repeating the same season over and over again.

"To everything, there is a season and a time to every purpose under the heavens" *(Ecclesiastes 3:1).*

I want to walk you through my 21-day journey of hearing and listening to the voice of God.

At the beginning of my journey, I fought the season of brokenness with great will power. I didn't want to get out of bed. I didn't want to go anywhere or see anyone. Once I opened my heart and listened for the voice of God, he helped me fight this battle.

There was a war going on in my mind. My spirit man was under attack, but that's when God brought deliverance. My nearly month-long journey to hearing and listening to God's voice helped me through the feelings of disappointment and failure.

My experience in hearing God's voice enabled me to win this seasonal battle with brokenness. My life was in turmoil, but as the Lord spoke, I went to the word of God. His words are quick, powerful, and sharper than any two-edged sword, piercing through the dividing asunder of soul and spirit, and the joints and marrow *(Hebrews 4:12).* God is a discerner of the heart's thoughts and intents. I'm sharing my story, so you can see how broken pieces can be restored with the guidance and humbleness of the calm voice of God, with no guilt or shame. I challenge you to take my experience and live it like your own. You're not alone; with prayer, all things are possible.

The Good News Bible refers to this phenomenon in the passage, "For the word of God is alive and active, sharper than any double-edged sword. It cuts all the way through, to where soul and spirit meet, to where joints and marrow come together. It judges the desires and thoughts of the heart" *(Hebrews 4:12).*

I needed God's word to go deep down into my soul, so my spirit man could be healed. I needed him to save me from this place of brokenness and overwhelming sorrow.

Regardless of the problem or situation, God has the amazing ability to do quick work in your innermost being. His word is alive and will minister to your soul and spirit. He searches through your heartfelt desires and awakens your soul.

The Living Bible explains the power of God's word in the following passage: "For whatever God says to us is full of living power; it is sharper than the sharpest dagger, cutting swift and deep into our innermost thoughts and desires with all their parts, exposing us for what we are" *(Hebrews 4:12).*

God's word penetrates our inner being, then it discerns and defines between spirit and soul. These represent our thoughts, emotions, desires, and choices. Our hearts can be softened and changed, so we may enter into God's rest. Or our hearts can be hardened against God's word, and we're condemned by the word and perish because of unbelief.
We know the promises of God are always yea and amen. His word brings healing and life to those who hear and submit to his word; it pronounces judgment on those who disregard it.

God gives hope to the hopeless; if you come to him asking, seeking, knocking, or calling out for help, he'll answer your cry. I gave in to God's will and rid myself of disobedience and stubbornness. I stopped running in the opposite direction of God's plans. Instead of fulfilling my desires, I caved to his will and accepted my known sins in life. That was the moment he blessed me and helped me win the war in my head. Not only did God heal me, but he also made me whole again.

I'm not sure where you are in your spiritual life. I know from experience when you starve your spirit man, your physical man will die. Get your bibles and meditate on God's word with me. Listen carefully to what the Lord says about whatever situation you're dealing with, whether it's heartache, devastation, brokenness, loneness, or bareness. The word of God is your answer about all aspects concerning your life and your future.

This level of transformation did not take place in 21 days for me; one day with the Lord may encompass a thousand years, and a thousand years may only represent one day *(Peter 3:8)*. No, we don't have a thousand years to live, the Lord views time from the perspective of eternity. What the Lord can accomplish in one day would take us a thousand years, but always remember the word of the Lord is nigh thee; for the word of the Lord is right and all his works are done in truth *(Psalm 33:4)*. God is never in a hurry, but he is always on time.

Don't allow time to defeat you because God is outside of time. God is eternal; it's never too late for God.

Every time I heard his voice, I opened my ears and let the Lord's voice ease my soul and give me direction.

Hearing the voice of God made me realize no one could conceal sin from God. If you're trying to do so, it'll cause you to lose some of the benefits he has for you. These benefits might include health, peace of mind, happiness, contentment, joy, and prosperity. Attempting to hide your sins may also drown you in guilt and inner torment. I thank God for giving me an ear to hear. I have no more guilt or shame, and my generational curses have been broken. I must say that this didn't happen without some rebuke, corrections, and edification in his word. Because of this experience, I'm free to be who God called me to be.

The devil doesn't always want to kill us. Sometimes, he just wants to torment us. This torment often starts in your mind. At times, you'll have to encourage yourself in the Lord. Remember, this battle is not ours alone. The Lord will guide you through your battle so long as you trust him. You must believe in him and never succumb to doubt. If you do this, you can come through the battle as pure gold.

"He has given me beauty for ashes and oil of joy for mourning. The garment of praise for the spirit of heaviness. I am a tree that the Lord himself has planted" *(Isaiah 61:1–3)*

Beauty for ashes represents a restored crown of beauty that has been exchanged for my ashes.

Oil represents God's special favor and lavish blessing through the anointing of his spirit upon my body, mind, and spirit.

This journal is all about me and the struggles I had. I'll explain how God ministered to me through the Holy Spirit and how I encouraged myself in the Lord. I've been encouraged in the Lord because I'm now sensitive to his voice.

NO MORE CHAINS ARE HOLDING ME.

Tawana,

.

God's Plan

Day 1

What do you require of me? I asked God, while feeling broken, alone, and shattered. I was in a very low place because I thought I heard the wrong thing from God. I prayed and prayed, *Lord, it is not my will but your will.*

"What do you require from me?" At about three in the morning, I received a response.

"Do Justly, to love mercy and to walk humbly with your God" *(Micah 6:8b)*. I paraphrased the Living Bible from memory in my head, "No, he has told you what he wants, and this is all it is: to be fair and just and merciful and to walk humbly with your God."

I thought I was already doing this; after all, I left family, friends, and my home to do what God wanted me to do. At that time, though, I was doing church work but not the work of the Lord.

I asked myself, *how do I do this?*

Not with sacrifices or other religious rituals *(Deuteronomy 10:12)*. Israel thought they could please God with sacrifices, hoping he would then leave them alone. But sacrifices and other religious rituals aren't enough; God wants changed lives. Similar to the way he called to Israel to have changed lives, he was asking for that same standard from me, and us. He doesn't want religious rituals.

He wants his people to be fair. Are you fair when you deal with people? Are you putting others before yourself?

He wants his people to love merrily. Do you show mercy to those who wrong you? Are you holding grudges? He wants love that comes from the heart. Faith and love from the heart are the keys to your relationship with God.

He wants humility. God opposes the proud, but he increases grace to the humble (James 4:6). We walk in humility by:

1) submitting ourselves unto God,
2) by resisting the devil,
3) by drawing nigh (close, near) to God
4) with clean hands and purified hearts *(James 4:6-8).*

God wants us to be living sacrifices. "I beseech you therefore, brethren, by the mercies of God, that you present your bodies a living sacrifice, holy, acceptable to God, which is your reasonable service. And do not be conformed to this world, but be transformed by the renewing of your mind, that you may prove what that good and acceptable and perfect will of God is" *(Romans 12:1,2).*

God has good, acceptable, and perfect plans for his children. He wants us to be transformed people with renewed minds, living to honor and obey him. He wants only what is best for us, and because he gave his son to make our new lives possible, we should joyfully give ourselves as living sacrifices for his service.

Christians are called to "not be conformed to this world," with its behavior and customs that are usually selfish and often corrupted. We must wisely decide that the world's behavior is off-limits. These behaviors include drinking, smoking, cursing, and adultery—all those unholy actions in the world). "We must go deeper than behavior and customs. It must be firmly planted in our minds by the renewing of your mind" *(Romans 12:2).*

It's possible to avoid most worldly customs and still be proud, covetous, selfish, stubborn, and arrogant. It's only when the Holy Spirit renews, reeducates, and redirects our minds are we truly transformed.

God doesn't want us just doing religious deeds but living *rightly.* "Circumcise yourselves to the Lord, and take away the foreskins of your hearts, You men of Judah and inhabitants of Jerusalem, lest my fury comes forth like fire, and burn so that no one can quench it, because of the evil of your doings" *(Jeremiah 4:4).*

Circumcision cuts away the flesh that could hold disease in its fold; it's the same as the heart that needs to be cleansed from sin's deadly disease. The essential surgery needs to happen on the inside, too. God calls for us to take away fleshly things that keep the heart from being spiritually devoted to him and from the true faith in him and his will.

I was doing religious deeds. We've tried all kinds of ways to please God, but God has made his wish clear; he wants his people to be just, merciful, and walk humbly with him.

True faith in God generates kindness, compassion, justice, and humility. That's what the Lord requires.

I've learned to be just, treating others fairly; merciful, showing compassion towards others; and to walk humbly with God daily.

Prayer

Father God, forgive me for having a form of godliness, forgive me for not being kind, compassionate, and forgive me for my prideful ways. Thank you for circumcising my heart to be spiritually devoted to you and walk-in true faith in you and your will. You said if I confess my sins, you're faithful and will forgive and cleanse me from all unrighteousness. Here I am, Lord. I humbly confess my sins to you, this day and every day of my life. In the mighty name of Jesus Christ, I pray.

Amen.

Free to Give

Day 2

*D*on't give out of necessity. I'd given so much, yet it felt like it wasn't enough. When I heard the Lord say, "Don't give out of necessity." I thought to myself, that's not me. I was in total denial. When you are faced with the truth, you either accept it or keep living in denial. Everything we own belongs to the Lord; what we do possess is not our own, but what God has entrusted to us. We've no rightful ownership over our possessions.

God loves a cheerful giver.

But this I say, he which soweth sparingly shall also reap sparingly; and he which soweth bountifully shall also reap bountifully. Every man according as he purposeth in his heart, so let him give not grudgingly or of necessity; for God loveth a cheerful giver *(II Corinthians 9:7)*.

According to II Corinthians 9:6, you can give either sparingly or bountifully, and God will reward you accordingly. The person who sows few seeds will have a small crop; the one who sows many seeds will have a large crop. It's not the quantity you give, but the quality of your heart, desires, sacrifice, and motives. The poor widow in Luke 21:1-4, in comparison to the rich men, had given more than all of them because her heart represented generous and extravert giving compared to the men who had much.

And God can make all grace abound toward you; that ye always having all sufficiency in all things may abound to every good work *(II Corinthians 9:6-8)*.

Decide within your heart to serve God and not mammon (money) *(Matthew 6:19-24)*. The word of God is clear that any greed is a form of idolatry *(Col 3:5)*. Idolatry allows material things to become the focus of our desires and values and replaces Christ as the Lord of our lives.

Give generously.

According to Luke 6:38 Good News Bible, "Give, and it shall be given unto you; good measure, pressed down, and shaken together, and running over, shall men give unto your bosom. For with the same measure that ye mete withal, it shall be measured to you again." Here, it's telling us how to give and that God will measure our giving and, in return, will give it to us.

Good measures.

God will do the measuring; you'll receive a full measure, a generous helping poured into your hands. The measure you use for others is the one God will use for you.

It'11 be pressed down—When you press something down, it makes room for more; therefore, God will pour more in.

Running over—Your blessings will be running over; you'll not have to run after it because men shall give into your bosom. People will start to bless you, and it's a payment from God for your generous giving.

Give to your Shepard.

"Let the elders that rule well be counted worthy of double honor, especially they labor in the word and doctrine. For the scripture saith, thou shalt not muzzle the ox that treaded out the corn. And the laborer is worthy of his reward" *(I Timothy 5:17-18)*.

Often, we're told what to give or give out of guilt, but God does not want us to give out of necessity. He wants us to be cheerful givers. Pray to God about what to give and whom to give to. He will never stir you wrong. After all, he wants to bless and prosper you.

According to I Timothy 5:17-18:

1) The elders who do good work as leaders should be considered worthy of

receiving double pay, especially those who work hard at preaching and teaching. This scripture is clearly saying to give to them.

2) You should never be made to feel guilty about what you're giving.

3) Give from your heart; God sees the heart.

4) Give as God has prospered you.

Most importantly, give as unto the Lord. "Every man shall give as they are able, of the Lord thy God which he hath given thee" (Deuteronomy 16:17).

Tithing is non-negotiable; some say tithing was for those in the Old Testament. That's not so; tithing has not changed.

In the Old Testament, the tithe amounted to one-tenth. Giving less than that was disobedient to God's law and was robbing God *(Mal 3:8-10).*

The New Testament requires our giving be in proportion to what God has given us. According to I Cor 16:2, "Upon the first day of the week let every one of you lay by him in store, as God hath prospered him, that there be no gatherings when I come." This does not mean you don't give God what he's requiring. If you can only give 10 percent, give 10 percent. If the Lord has prospered you to give more than 10 percent, give more.

In Matthew 22:21, Jesus says, "Render therefore unto Cesar the things which are Cesar's and unto God the things that are God's." God is a God of order, and things are always put into perspective: their proper place. Cesar represents the government. They've taxed us and told us what we would give and don't give us a choice; they take it. God gives us a choice.

Some blessings and curses go with tithing. It's our choice. When you don't tithe, you're cursed with a curse *(Malachi 3:9).* You have a curse on top of a curse.

Blessings

This is the only time that God says to prove him *(Malachi 3:10).* He's saying trust me and watch what I'll do for you. Often, we don't trust God because our eyes are on man. Don't worry about what they're doing; God will repay them.

When you tithe, he'll open up the window of heaven and pour you out a blessing that 'you'll not have room enough to receive it *(Malachi 3:10).* The blessings that come with faithfulness in financial giving will come both in this life and in the life hereafter.

He'll rebuke the devourer for your sakes, he shall not destroy the fruits of your ground, and your vine shall not cast her fruit before the time *(Malachi 3:11)*. The devourer in this passage is anything or anyone who tries to eat up your harvest: someone who eats greedily or voraciously.

All nations will call you to bless, and you'll be a delightsome land *(Malachi 3:12)*.

Don't worry about what people say or how they try to make you feel. If you're giving according to God's word, let him repay you for your giving. God has promised to reward us according to how we have given to him. Give according to the word of God and do it cheerfully.

Once I started giving according to his word, I had no more guilt about giving. After all, giving is a form of worship; when I give, I worship the Lord in my giving.

Prayer

Father God, I thank you for your word, for your word is true and quick and powerful and sharper than any two-edged sword. Thank you for giving me revelation on giving, for you love a cheerful giver. You said to give, and it shall be given unto me, pressed down, shaken together, running over, and men shall give into my bosom. Thank you, God, that the wealth of the sinner is laid up for the just and that the blessings of the Lord make it rich and added no sorrow to it. Thank you for your total health, wealth, and prosperity. It's in the matchless name of Jesus Christ, I pray.

Amen.

Building a
New Foundation

Day 3

*H*eaven is my throne, and the earth is my footstool. Where is the house that ye build unto me? And where is the place of my rest? (Isaiah 66:1, Acts 7:49.) I didn't know where these words came from or why the Lord spoke. I knew at that point that it was something in the subconscious of my mind.

When the Lord told me to leave my place of worship, I was confused. I didn't think the place he told me to go to was fit for us to worship our Lord and Savior. This bothered me. I kept praying, asking the Lord for resources to build up his house. He didn't give it to me. One night, I pondered, *"why didn't he do it?* Then, I heard: "Heaven is my throne, and the Earth is my footstool. Where is the house that ye build unto me? And where is the place of my rest?" It startled and shocked me. Then, I began to search the scriptures.

The Living Bible paraphrases what I heard well in the passage: "Heaven is my throne, and the Earth is my footstool: What Temple can you build for me as good as that? My hand has made both Earth and skies, and they're mine. Yet, I'll look with pity on the man who trembles at my word" *(Isaiah 66:1-2).*

My heart was ready to build, but my time was not properly aligned with his word. God is not impressed with any building that humans construct for him, but he does delight in those who are humble in spirit, who rely on God's help, and who follow his word with all their hearts *(Isaiah 57:15)*. In essence, these people humble themselves to God. God promises to dwell with those who have a contrite and humble spirit.

Contrite refers to those who are brokenhearted because of their sinfulness or the enemy's oppression and who cry out to God for deliverance.

Humble spirit refers to those who are humble or bowed down by adversity.

This was when I gave it up (and didn't worry about what folks said or thought). I had to get my soul right, so I could serve him in spirit and truth.

My husband thought I had lost my mind, but I was free. I had permission from the one that mattered, and there was no looking back.

Stephen was accused of speaking against the temple, a holy place *(Acts 6:13)*. Stephen knew the temple's importance; he also knew that the highest didn't dwell in temples made by hands. God is not limited; he lives in a place of worship place but can also go wherever hearts of faith are opened to receive him.

God wants to live in us. We go to church, a physical building to worship, where we enter to worship and depart to serve. Our temples, such as our bodies, mind, and hearts, are not clean; our bodies are the temple of the Holy Ghost. "What? Know ye not that your body is the temple of the Holy Ghost, which is in you, which ye have of God, and ye are not your own?" *(I Corinthians 6:19)*. Our bodies are the Holy Spirit's dwelling place because the spirit lives in us and we belong to God. So, your body must never be defiled by any impurity or evil.

Often, we look at defiling our temples by adultery, fornication, etc. It also includes thoughts, desires, deeds, overeating, etc. These are actions and behaviors we normally don't see on the outside.

We must live in such a way to honor and please God with our bodies.

Stephen was an excellent example; although he was martyred, lives were still saved. Saul (later converted to Paul) was one of the ones who consented to his stoning; Saul witnessed the Glory of God and was later saved and went on to become one of the greatest apostles of Jesus Christ *(Acts, chapters 6-9)*.

Remember, he's coming back for a church without spot or wrinkle (that's us, not the building). Draw nigh unto God and develop an intimate relationship with him. He wants to live in us, so others can be saved.

Prayer

Father God, I humbly submit to you. Forgive me for not taking care of my temple and having an unclean temple. You said our bodies are the temple of the Holy Ghost. Holy Spirit, help me to honor my body and forgive me for having more respect for a building and not for you.

Father, you said you're nigh unto them who are of a broken heart and saveth, such as be of a contrite spirit. Holy Spirit, you're welcome, have your way in my life, lead and guide me, teach me how to have an intimate relationship with God.

It's in the matchless name of Jesus Christ, I pray.
Amen.

His Way, My Will

Day 4

*W*hat have I commissioned you to do? I was still asking. What do you want me to do? Then, I heard: "What have I commissioned you to do?" His question was plain and simple. "Go ye, therefore, teach all nations, baptizing them in the name of the Father, and the Son, and the Holy Ghost. Teaching them to observe all things whatsoever I have commanded you; and lo I am with you always, even unto the end of the world, Amen" *(Matthew 28:19,20)*.
Often, we want to follow our agendas, but the plan has already been before us. It's very plain and simple. This is why we're frustrated and always in someone else's affairs.

One of the keys to my breakthrough was being focused on what the Lord said. I didn't need to look to the right or the left to see who was sitting next to me. I can't say what the Lord is calling you to do. I heard him plain as day, "Go ye therefore and teach all nations baptizing them in the name of the Father and Son, and the Holy Ghost. Teaching them to observe all things whatsoever I have commanded you; and lo I am with you always, even unto the end of the world" *(Matthew 28:19,20)*.

Preach the gospel—the good news of the death, burial, and resurrection of Jesus Christ—by the power of the Holy Ghost *(Ephesians 3:20)*. This enables us to make other disciples. Preach even when they don't want to hear you preach. The bibles say one plant, another water, but it's God who gives the increase (*I Corinthians 3:6*).

Baptize them in the name of the Father and of the Son and of the Holy Ghost (not you actually doing the baptizing), but our preaching/teaching should be so affected that we win souls for Christ and lead them to the Shephard to be baptized. Baptism is an outward sign of an inward change by one who has accepted Jesus Christ as their savior *(Romans 6:6; Acts 2:38; Colossians 2:11-12; I Corinthians 12:3; I Peter 3:21)*.

Teach them to observe all things. Once they accept Christ and are baptized, we teach them to grow stronger in his word. They start as newborn babes, desiring the sincere milk of the word. Then, they grow from babies in Christ to fully mature Christians who can lead others to Christ *(I Peter 2:2)*.

We should be fishers of men, as Jesus instructed Simon Peter in Matthew 4:19. We all have different titles, positions, and assignments in the kingdom. There are no little chiefs of big chiefs in the sight of God; we're all equal, just doing different things in the kingdom and as unto the Lord. Our one common goal is to win souls for Christ. Whatever your calling or assignment is, let your light shine before men, so they may see your good works and glorify your Father who is in heaven *(Matthew 5:16)*.

According to Ephesians 4:11-12, he gave apostles, prophets, evangelists, pastors, and teachers the job of perfecting the saints and edifying the body of Christ. This was their ministry's work.

Apostles: Commissioned by the resurrected Lord to establish the church *(Acts 4:33-37)*.

Prophets: Are those who speak under the Holy Spirit's inspiration, who bring a message from God to the church *(Romans 12:6)*.

Evangelists: Those gifted by God to proclaim the gospel to the unsaved *(Ephesians 4:11)*.

Pastors: Those chosen and gifted to oversee the church and care for its spiritual needs *(Acts 14:23)*.

Teachers: Those gifted to clarify and explain God's word to build up the church (Romans 12:7).

We're many members in one body, and all members do not have the same office. We all have our place, and we should be glorifying the father by winning souls. We should be baptizing all nations in the name of the Father, and the Son, and the Holy Ghost. We should be teaching them to observe all things, whatsoever we've commanded. The Lord is with me even unto the end of the world. Amen.

Prayer

Most holy and everlasting Father forgive me for not doing what you called me to do. Holy Spirit, I have you on the inside of me to be my helper and my guide. Lead and guide me and help me to do what you've commissioned me to do. Help me to live a life that will win souls for Christ. Teach me how to be fishers of men. Help me to let my light shine that men may see my good works and glorify my Father in heaven. It's in the matchless name of Jesus Christ, I pray.

Amen.

God's Protection

Day 5

*M*y hands are upon you. In the middle of the day, that's what I heard the Lord say to me.

People say they're with you, but then they try to tear you down in secret. When I heard God's words, "My hands are upon you," I knew no one could harm me—not even the devil and his angels. After all, the Lord is on my side; I will not fear: what can man do unto me? (Psalm 118:6).

Because the Spirit of the Lord is upon me, he hath anointed me to preach the gospel to the poor; he hath sent me to heal the broken-hearted, to preach deliverance to the captives, to recover sight to the blind, to set at liberty them who are bruised and to preach the acceptable year of the Lord *(Luke 4:18,19.)*

When the Lord's hands are upon us, Satan can see it because he once lived in the presence of God. He'll use people, especially those closest to us, to break you, hurt you, and leave you wondering, *is the Lord really with me?*

He says in I John 4:4, "Ye are of God, little children, and have overcome them; because greater is he that is in you than he that is in the world."

The Good News Bible says: "But you belong to God, my children, and have defeated the false prophets because the Spirit who is in you is more powerful than the spirit in those who belong to the world."

The Lord's hands are upon me. He has called me to share his ministry in the same ways he did. This doesn't mean when people fit us into their agenda for their profit or gain, rather it's when the Holy Spirit directs you to share his ministry.

He has called me:

To preach the gospel to the poor (those crushed in spirit, the broken-hearted).
To heal (those who are bruised and oppressed spiritually and physically).
To open the spiritual eyes of those blinded by what the world and Satan offer, to see the good news of the gospel (death, burial, and resurrection of Jesus Christ).

To proclaim the time of true freedom and salvation from sin, fear, and guilt. Whom the Son sets free is free indeed. I'll never be ashamed of who I am in Christ, even when people accept me. I know the hands of the Lord are upon me.

He said in Isaiah 41:10 NIV, "So do not fear, for I am with you; do not be dismayed, for I am your God. I will strengthen you and help you; I will uphold you with my righteous right hand."

With the power of the Holy Ghost, we can reach new levels because God's hands are upon us.

Prayer

Father God, thank you for your steadfast love and comfort, knowing your hands are upon me. Thank you for always causing me to triumph in victory. It's through your love, peace, and joy that I walk in. Father, thank you for choosing me; use me for your glory. I rest in you, in the mighty name of Jesus Christ, I pray.

Amen.

New Vision

Day 6

Blinded eyes open. At times, I felt like God could not use me because of my weaknesses, but God uses us even through our weakness because his strength is greater than our strengths.

Why do we live in the shadows of others? Or by what we've heard others say to us, even our parents?

"You can't do this."

"You'll never amount to anything."

"You're ugly."

"You're fat."

"You're skinny."

"You have a big nose."

"You're too dark."

"You're too light."

"You're nobody."

"Be Quiet."

"You're stupid."

The list goes on and on. We hear and remember these harsh words. So, when we try to do something, we hear those voices taunting us.

If the blind man in Luke 18 had listened to the people, he would've died blind. By faith, he cried out unto Jesus, "Thou son of David, have mercy on me." That's all the father wants from us. He wants us to cry out to him. Jesus asked him, "What do you want from me?" *(Luke 18:40b GNB).*

When blinded eyes are opened,

we see things differently. Our relationship with the Lord is different.

We now see that we have to give a personal account for ourselves. It doesn't matter what others say or do; you're responsible for yourself.

Forgive, love, and treat others the way Christ treated you. He loved us so much that he forgave others even on the cross. He loved us so much that he endured a punishment that should have been for us.

Love, as Christ has commanded us to do. I give unto you a new commandment that ye love one another; as I have loved you, you also love one another. By this shall all men know that ye are my disciples; if ye have love one to another (John 13: 34,35).

When the blinded eye is opened,

we walk differently. Jesus said in John 8:12, "I am the light of the world; he that followeth me shall not walk in darkness but shall have the light of life. We are a light that sits on a hill. When we become followers of Jesus Christ, we're delivered from the darkness of sin, the world, and Satan. Our walk is different; we're in the world, but not of the world.

When blinded eyes are opened,

Our praise is different. In everything, give praise, through the good praise God. When we're happy, we must praise God. When we're sad, we must praise God.

Why? Like the psalmist said, "I once was lost, but now I'm found, was blind, but now I see" (Citation). When we start to see through the eyes of Jesus Christ, everything looks different.

When blinded eyes are opened,

We see people differently. We no longer view people as a race, color, or a different denomination but as a child of the highest God. Instead of shutting people out, we have to be like Jesus to deal with the sin. Every person that Jesus encountered, if they had sin in their life, he dealt with the sin.

When blinded eyes are opened,

We don't view our circumstances the same; our circumstances look different, because we as Paul says, have the assurance of this. And we know that all things work together for good to those who love God, to them who are the called according to his purpose. (Romans 8:28).
When Jesus, the Son of David, opens your eyes, you can no longer be the same physically or spiritually.

Paul, formerly Saul, had a different encounter than what the blind man had. His eyes were opened naturally and spiritually, and his life was no longer the same. Let the scales fall off your eyes so you can see. Once the scales fell off my eyes, my once blinded eyes could see again.

Prayer

Father God, thank you for removing the scales from my eyes. Holy Spirit, help me to never be in darkness again. I know the enemy comes to steal, kill, and destroy. Jesus, you said I might have life and have it more abundantly. Thank you for allowing me to see others the way you see them. I bless you for your touch and for loving me so much that you removed the scales from my eyes. Order my steps daily and show me where you're at work so I can join you. In the name of Jesus Christ, I pray.
Amen.

God's Honor

Day 7

*P*raise Ye the Lord *(Psalm 146)*. I was hearing this all day. This was a day of **PRAISE**. Guess what? You can depend on God because it's temporary and often unreliable when you depend on a man. Help from God is always lasting and whole. **Praise Ye the Lord**.

We're all going through something, but verse three of this same Psalm says: "Put not your trust in princes, nor in the son of man in whom there is no hope, so put your hope in the right place."

I don't know where you are in your spiritual walk, what you're going through or how you feel after six days of hearing the voice of God. But the psalmist starts off Psalm 146 with the passage: **"Praise ye the Lord. Praise the Lord O, my soul."** If you're still reading this, you're still alive. So, you have a lot to praise the Lord about. **Praise ye the Lord.**

When we put our hope and trust in God, it's a guaranteed winner.

God will execute judgment for the oppressed *(Psalm 146:7a).* Oppressed means to be subject to harsh and severe treatment but still **praise ye the Lord.** Hannah, who was barren, was oppressed by her adversary Peninnah *(I Samuel 1:6)*. If you read 1 Peter 5:8, the adversary is described as the devil, walking about seeking whom he may devour. He can't devour everybody; that's why he's seeking whom he may devour. Psalm 146:7a says God will execute judgment for the oppressed. If you read the entire sequence of events in 1 Samuel Chapter 1, you'll see that God executed judgment on behalf of Hannah; after all, her bareness is a direct activity of God. Hannah's barrenness, frustration, shame, and waiting were a test of her faith. Hannah was barren and couldn't have children. What's your barrenness, or unproductiveness? God is no respecter of persons: **praise ye the Lord.**

Whatever it is, you have the choice of how you're going to handle it. I encourage you to **praise ye the Lord**. If you read 1 Samuel, chapter 1 in its entirety, you see that Hannah goes to the Lord, prays, and worships the Lord. Her worship was a token of the moment she realized she could trust in God.

She was assured in her heart that God heard her prayer. Hannah received new strength; the Lord gave her Samuel, three more sons, and two daughters. God will execute judgment for the oppressed. **Praise ye the Lord**.

He gives food to the hungry. At times, we may have difficulties in our lives. We must learn to depend on God; just like he fed the children of Israel manna from on high, he'll do the same for us. **Praise ye the Lord,** who daily loads us with benefits *(Psalm 68:19)*. Man shall not live by bread alone but by every word that comes from the mouth of God *(Matthew 4:4)*. **Praise ye the Lord.**

He loses the prisoner. Prisoners are legally held in prison as a punishment for crimes they've committed or are waiting for their outcome. Just like Paul and Silas while in prison, at midnight, they prayed and sang praises unto God. There was a great earthquake, and all the doors were opened immediately *(Acts 16:23-40)*. **Praise ye the Lord.**

Open the eyes of the blind. In Matthew 9:27-31, Jesus heals two men who were blind. Blind Bartimaeus received his sight *(Mark 10:46-52)*. Our eyes can also be opened spiritually. While Paul was on the road of Damascus, he was struck blind only to receive spiritual eyes by Jesus Christ *(Acts 9:1-16)*. **Praise ye the Lord.**

Those that are bowed or bent down vs. 8. The Lord will raise you. The woman in Luke 13:11 had a Spirit of Infirmity for 18 years and was bowed down. She couldn't lift herself. When Jesus saw her, he called her to him and said, "Woman, thou art loosed from thy infirmity." Jesus laid his hands on her, and immediately she was made **straight**. She glorified God. **Praise ye the Lord.**

Loves the righteous vs. 8, The eyes of the Lord are upon the righteous, and his ears are open unto their cry *(Psalm 34:15)*. Enoch, a righteous man did not see death; and Abraham, a righteous man, became the father of many nations. Nobody but the righteous shall see God. He protects those who are righteous; he allows them to rule like kings and lets them be honored forever. *(Job 36:7 GNB)*. **Praise ye the Lord.**

Preserve the strangers vs. 9; We're to express God's love by our kindness and generosity to others. He warned the children of Israel not to treat strangers unfairly. They were strangers in the land of Egypt *(Exodus 22:21)*. We're reminded in Hebrews 13:2 to be not forgetful to entertain strangers; for thereby, some have entertained angels unawares. **Praise ye the Lord.**

Gives hope to the fatherless and the widows vs. 9. God in his holy habitation will be a father to the fatherless and a judge of the widows *(Psalm 68:5)*. God takes delight in protecting the weak, disadvantaged, wronged, and lonely among his people. If you feel alone, seek God's protection because the fatherless and widows are under special protection from God. **Praise ye the Lord.**

But the way of the wicked he turns upside down (Psalm 146:9).

Hope in the Lord is a sure and steadfast anchor for the soul. We praise God for his splendor, glory, majesty, and beauty. He's the one who created the heavens and the Earth.

After the children of Israel crossed the red sea, a great cry of praise went up from the people of God *(Exodus 15:1-21)*. The book of revelation tells us that in the end, those who get the victory over the beast are given harps by God himself, and they sing in God's immediate presence "the song of Moses" and the song of the lamb, which represent triumph *(Revelations 15:3)*.

If your hope is in the Lord, it's a sure thing *(Hebrews 6:19)*.

The psalmist concludes that "The Lord shall reign forever, even thy God, O Zion, unto all generations" *(Psalm 146:10)*. **Praise ye the Lord.**

If you find yourself in any of the categories above, **praise ye the Lord**. He'll give you hope.

We sing the song "Praise is what I do," but is it really what we do? Normally, for some of us, including me. Once God delivers us from a circumstance or an issue, that's when we praise him after he has delivered us. We have to learn how to give God an anyhow praise. Don't wait until after you've come out. Praise him in advance. We're victorious in the Lord. **Praise ye the Lord.**

Praise comes from a Latin word meaning "value or price." When you give praise to God, you're proclaiming his merit and worth. God is the only one worthy of our praise.

Israel's children praised God after they crossed the red sea. After three days, there was no water. Instead of praising God, they murmured and complained, but God provided water for them anyway. That's one of the reasons we must praise him. He's a merciful God. Not only will he feed the hungry, but he'll also provide water for the thirsty. Yet we say, "Praise is what I do."

If we're praising instead of mumbling and complaining, we would know "it is of the Lord's mercies that we are not consumed because his compassions fail not. They are new every morning; great is thy faithfulness" *(Lamentations 3:22-23).*

Praise ye the Lord.

That's why David said, "I will bless the Lord at all times; his praises will continually be in my mouth. My soul shall make her boast in the Lord, and the humble shall hear thereof. Oh, magnify the Lord with me" *(Psalm 34:1-3).*

David knew God's presence was full of joy and pleasures forevermore at his right hand *(Psalm 16:11)*. **Praise ye the Lord.**

Paul continues with this same mindset. In Ephesians 5:19, he tells us to speak to ourselves in psalms, hymns, and spiritual songs because singing makes melody in your heart to the Lord. If you can't say it out loud, say it in your heart. **Praise ye the Lord.**

Let everything that has breath praise ye the Lord.

Praise ye the Lord.

Prayer:

Father, I bless you and praise your holy name because you inhabit the praises of your people. I bless you, Lord, with the fruit of my lips and the sincerity of my heart. Bless the Lord oh my soul and all that's within me. I bless your holy name. There is no other name that is worthy of all the praise, honor, and glory. I'll keep praise on my lips, through the good and bad because it's you who gives me hope. In the matchless name of Jesus Christ, I pray. Amen.

Making Moves

Day 8

*G*o forward and keep moving. The enemy tried to make me look back, but I heard, *"Go forward and keep moving."*

Satan may be out of the garden, but he still finds his way into the vulnerable areas of our lives. We have to remember God is with us, even in times of sinful temptation. He's promised to give us the power to withstand such moral crises.

Just like the Lord was fighting for the children of Israel, he has fought for us. He took the sting from death, defeated Satan, and sat at our father's right hand, making intercession on our behalf. We must go forward and keep moving.

When Adam messed up in the garden of Eden, it seemed as though there was no hope. In Genesis 3:15, God gave us a promise; he said, "And I will put enmity between thee and the woman, and between thy seed and her seed; it shall bruise thy head, and thou shalt bruise his heel." This is the first promise of God's plan of redemption for us.

God promised Christ would be born of a woman, He would be bruised through his crucifixion, but he would be raised from the dead to destroy Satan, sin, and death.

When Christ got up, the battle was won. We have the victory; we have to keep it moving and go forward.

Satan knows he's lost, but he's still trying to get us to give up on God. This isn't anything new. The enemy goes to and fro, seeking whom he may devour; he tried it on Job. Satan thought for sure Job would curse God to his face *(Book of Job)*. He lost then, and he's losing now.

When he taught his disciples, he told them in Luke 17:32, "Remember Lot's wife." In her disobedience, Lot's wife looked back; instead of going forward, she looked back and was turned into a pillar of salt. She looked back because her heart was still in Sodom. Sodom represented: "Wickedness (the opposite of righteousness), homosexuality, injustice, immorality, worldly possessions, a total lack of trust in God."

What's tugging at our hearts, tempting us not to move forward? Could we be like:

Lot's wife, she couldn't let go of what she was leaving behind in Sodom and Gomorrah, or

The Children of Israel, who knew the acts of God but not his ways? They saw and knew the miracles of God, but they didn't know the ways of God, or
Do we value the wickedness of the world we are in, and our possessions are more valuable than the commandment of God?

If you look around, we live in a modern-day Sodom and Gomorrah. We're in this world but not of this world. We're just pilgrims passing through; we should look to the hills from where our help comes. All of our help comes from the Lord *(Psalm 121:2)*.

Are we attached to our Lord and Savior Jesus Christ and the hope of his return? If we're to go forward, there is hope in knowing the King is on his way back soon. Keep moving and don't look back. The enemy is going to and fro as a roaring lion. The book of Job records how the Lord asked Satan, "Where are you going"? He said, "To and fro." Satan is the accuser of the brethren. Just like the accused Job, he's accusing us as well, but Jesus, who sits at the father's right hand, is making intercession on our behalf. His blood covers us; we have to be like Job, no matter what comes our way. We must have faith in God and keep moving.

We can't hold onto the past and expect to move forward in God. Stop looking back into the past. Stop looking back at what happened to us. Just move forward with God. God has great things in store for us, but we can't get those things if we keep holding onto the past.

Keep moving; keep pressing.

Prayer

Father God, thank you for the presence and power of the Holy Spirit, who helps me to keep it moving. Holy Spirit, help me to never want to go back. You said in your word that you order the steps of a good man, Lord, and he delighted in his way, lead me in the way you would have me to go. In the mighty name of Jesus Christ, I pray.

Amen.

Unmeasurable Love

Day 9

*G*od loves me deeply, after all. The spirit of shame was trying to come over me. I heard, "I love you deeply after all." Now, I can confidently walk with my head held high in Christ.

Don't let your past mistakes and failures define you. That is the voice of shame. You aren't what you've done or haven't done. You're not what's been done to you; you're whom God says you are, his child. The Lord says, "Yea I have loved thee with an everlasting love; therefore, with loving kindness have I drawn thee" *(Jeremiah 31:3b).*

We're fearfully and wonderfully made; marvelous are thy works (Psalm 139:14). I'm reminded in I Peter 2:9 that I'm a chosen generation, a royal priesthood, a holy nation, a peculiar people, that ye should shew forth the praises of him who hath called you out of darkness into his marvelous light.

I've been molested, abused, lied to, and taken advantage of. Despite all my misfortunes, **God loves me deeply** because before I was born, he ordained me in my mother's womb. "Before I formed thee in the belly, I knew thee; and before you camest forth out of the womb, I sanctified thee, and I ordained thee a prophet unto the nation" *(Jeremiah 1:5).*

"I chose you before I gave your life, and before you were born, I selected you to be a prophet to the nations *(Jeremiah 1:5 GNB).*

Although wc cnd up in a different place through our disobedience, God already knew what he ordained and destined us for. That's why we have to hear the voice of God and make sure what we do and say is what the Lord has ordained us to say and do.

A family member molested me; that was not God's plan for me. I allowed the voice of shame to overcome me. Instead of trusting my parents, I kept it to myself. When we keep these hurtful things to ourselves, the spirit of unforgiveness begins to creep in. I was holding these molestations in my heart for years. I had to open my mouth and forgive them. The forgiveness was not for them; it was for me.

Many people think molestation happens because you've done something wrong. Molestation, rape, and child pornography are all Spirits, and it's the same Spirits that were in the garden of Eden. Lust of the flesh, the lust of the eyes, and the pride of life.

Your flesh desires it; you just have to have it.

Your eyes see it and plant a seed.

You're too prideful to admit your shortcomings.

We must forgive them. We must pray these generational curses off us and our children. If I had to go down my family line, at least one other child had been molested or raped. We conceal it and keep it to ourselves, hoping no one will ever find out. These demons go through our family line and keep molesting and raping our daughters, and our sons become molesters and rapers. If we don't pray these demons out of our families, they'll try to destroy us.

David's son saw his sister, and she was beautiful to look upon. Then pride set in. Instead of asking his father to give her to him as his wife, he raped her. The same three spirits: lust of the flesh, the lust of the eyes, and the pride of life. Lusting after people and things could cause your demise.

Jacob's daughter – the young man saw her, desired, her and raped her.

Molestation and rape don't just happen at the hands of men, but women as well. I was molested by a man and a woman, which made me distrust both men and women. **God had to deliver me from me.**

I didn't trust anyone. If anyone tried to get close to me, I would pull away. I didn't fully trust my husband because of the things I experienced in my previous marriage. We were married for more than 10 years before I fully trusted him. The only reason I was able to reach that point in my marriage was because of the voice of God. He delivered me from me.

I heard the Spirit of the Lord say, **"I love you deeply after all."** It doesn't matter what I've been through or who hurt me. God loves me deeply after all, and I will not fear.

"So do not fear, for I am with you; do not be dismayed, for I am your God. I will strengthen you and help you; I will uphold you with my righteous right hand" (Isaiah 41:10 NIV).

God loves imperfect people.

Peter denied Christ three times. When the Lord spoke to Mary at the tomb, he said, "tell my disciples and Peter."

If God loves me deeply why do I have to forgive? In Matthew 18:21, Peter asked Jesus a question. Jesus responded in Matthew 18:22, "I say not unto thee, until seven times: but, until seventy times seven.

We have to keep on forgiving others. Jesus set the example of forgiveness. He loved us so much that he took a punishment he didn't deserve, and he knew no sin.

After all the hurt I've experienced and the hurt others experienced from me, why not forgive? I was a sinner saved by Grace (**G**od's **R**iches **A**t Christ's **E**xpense) and God forgave me (that's how much he loves me). If we're unmerciful and unforgiving toward others, it'll block the flow of God's forgiveness toward us. Paul tells us in Ephesians 4:31 and 32 to put away all bitterness, resentment, and animosity toward others. He tells us to be kind one to another, forgiving one another, even as God for Christ's sake forgave us.

God loves me deeply and to experience the true love of God I must walk in love. Love comes at a high price but it's worth it.

Forgiveness is not always easy, after all, look at what it caused Jesus. **"He loves me deeply afterwards."** It's childish to harbor, or hold on to, unforgiveness.

We must possess an attitude that desires to forgive and help those who offend us. We must avoid trying to get spiritual revenge or showing hatred. But we should not condone habitual sin.

• We must not allow anyone to mistreat or abuse us indefinitely.

• We must maintain an attitude that is always ready to help and forgive the offender.

Jesus tells us "woe unto the world because of offenses: for it must need be that offenses come, but woe to that man by whom the offenses cometh" *(Mathew 18:7).*

"How terrible for the world that there are things that make people lose their faith! Such things will always happen-but how terrible for the one who causes them." *(GNB).*

This is why we have to forgive. Jesus has already declared that those who are instrumental in placing sinful things before others and especially children will receive the ultimate condemnation. He says, "it was better for him that a millstone was hanged about his neck, and that he was drowned in the dept of the sea" *(Matthew 18:6).*

If you're dealing with any past hurts in your lives, especially things that happened as a child, forgive. The key to receiving forgiveness is admitting guilt and repenting. God is forgiving, and he will forgive all sins. Forgive and pray for those who have hurt you.

The Lord has me and he loves me deeply after all. When you know the greatness of God's love, your response is worship and praise. "I will praise you O Lord my God, with all my heart; I will glorify your name forever" *(Psalm 86:12).*
A lot of times, we grow up in a household full of turmoil, but we have to reprogram our lifestyles and get addicted to our inner peace. God has promised to give you his peace. This peace only comes from listening to what God, the Lord, says *(Psalm 85:8).*

Peace is connected with righteousness; righteousness and peace kiss each other *(Psalm 85:10).* Peace comes from living in the right relationship with God *(Romans 5:1).*

The Lord loves me deeply after all. So, find your peace with God.

$\backsim$

Prayer

Most holy and everlasting Father, thank you for revealing all unforgiveness, bitterness, and malice in my heart. Holy Spirit, search me, for you know what's in my heart and the secret thoughts of my mind reveal any hidden sins. Thank you, Lord, for loving me even when I didn't love myself. May your love be evident in my walk with you toward others. Thank you for healing me and setting me free. It's in the matchless name of Jesus Christ, I pray.

Amen.

Favor need to
be holded

Day 10

*W*ho God has blessed can't no man curse.

When the hands of God are on your life, no one can stop your blessings. It's like having a fence around you.

Why did I hear this particular phrase? I don't know. In a dream, the Lord showed how the enemy was trying to take me out. I was in the middle of an open field, and all around me were high iron poles. I felt like there was no escape. An angel arrived and gave me wings. The angel lifted me above everything blocking me from escaping. I could feel myself being lifted toward the heavens.

Those poles were darts of hatred, envy, jealousy, and unforgiveness. Each pole played a part in trying to hold me down. I won't be afraid of the terror by night nor the arrows that flieth by day *(Psalm 91:15)*.

Stop apologizing for how the Lord has blessed you. "The blessings of the Lord make it rich and add no sorrow to it" *(Proverbs 10:22)*.

Balak tried to curse the children of Israel. He consulted Balaam, a sorcerer, to curse the children of Israel. He thought Balaam had the power to turn God against his people, but who God has blessed no man can curse.

A sorcerer is a person who has magical powers. Someone who uses or practices magic that derives from supernatural or occult sources.

Balaam acknowledged the Lord was a powerful God. But he didn't believe in the Lord as the only true God. He had an outward disguise of spirituality, but his inward man and life were corrupt.

Isaiah 54:17 tells us, "No weapon that is formed against thee shall prosper; and every tongue that shall rise against thee in judgment thou shalt condemn. This is the heritage of the servants of the Lord, and their righteousness is of me, saith the Lord."

The Living Word Bible paraphrased the passage as: "But in that coming day, no weapon turned against you shall succeed, and Yahweh have justice against every courtroom lie. This is the heritage of the servants of the Lord. This is the blessing I have given you, says the Lord."

Yes, the weapons are going to form, but they won't prosper. He'll cut them down; it won't come to the past. He's even going to condemn those who raise their tongue or open their mouth against you. He has assured us this is our heritage, which has been given to us). God is going to fight for us.

There are people like Balaam today. They have wandered off the right road and followed the way of Balaam, who loved to earn money by doing wrong. But Balaam was stopped from his mad course when his donkey rebuked him with a human voice *(2 Peter 2:15,16)*.

Balaam traveled nearly 400 miles to curse Israel, which would equate to about a four-hour drive in our time. He traveled a long way to try and curse what God had blessed. Don't waste your time or your gas trying to stop what God has already blessed. Who God has blessed can't no man curse.

Balaam did what God told him to do for a time, but eventually, his evil motives and desire for money overpowered his actions. Don't let the greed for money, popularity, or your agenda make you think you can curse God's anointed. The Lord said in I Chronicles 16:22, "Touch not my anointed and do my prophets no harm." If God has anointed them, you can't curse them. When the hand of God is on your life, nobody can stop or block your blessings from the Lord, so you can't curse what God has blessed. As long as you're dancing to the beat of other folks' music, they don't have a problem with you. When you start to follow the voice of God, folks will want to curse you and write you off.

Be not dismayed: "The Lord is on my side; I will not fear; what can man do unto me?" *(Psalm118:6).*

Take refuge in the Lord. He is for you and with you. He gives you help and strength, so stop apologizing for who you are in the Lord. It doesn't matter if they lie to you or even speak ill against you. You have the promise, or the inheritance of the Lord. They won't prosper. The Lord is on your side.

Who God has blessed can't no man curse.

Prayer

Father God, I thank you in the name of Jesus Christ for having your hands upon me. Holy Spirit, help me to always look to the hills from where my help comes from. Thank you, Lord, my trust and strength are in you. Thank you for being an ever-loving and faithful God.

In the name of Jesus Christ, I pray.

Amen.

Intercessory Prayer

Day 11

*P*ray for one another. The thief cometh not, but for to steal, and to kill, and to destroy. Tearing each other down is one of the ways the enemy uses us, so we're not praying for each other. Jesus says, "I am come that they might have life, and that they might have it more abundantly" *(John 10:10).*

> *Jesus had an inner circle: Peter, James, and John. There wasn't any division or animosity among them on Jesus' part. He was a perfect role model. He taught them how to pray, how to win souls, and how to be a team. There was probably friction, but it wasn't at the hands of Jesus. Jesus was about his father's business*

> *He did not talk about the other disciples. He said what he had to say to them to their faces.*

> *"Peter before the cock crows thrice you will deny me three times" (Matthew 26:34).*

> *Simon, Simon, behold, Satan hath desired to have you, that he may sift you as wheat (Luke 22:31).*

All were at the last supper, including Judas, when he said one of you will betray me. They all asked, "Lord is it I?" Peter was a hot-headed person. If Jesus was talking about the others, do you think that Judas would have still been at the table?

Jesus was the exemplary leader:

"Jesus prayed for his disciples, and the ones to come (us)" *(John 17:1-25).*

Jesus' prayer for his disciples, and us, shows how much he cared for us both then and now. We must have the same passion. Jesus is our greatest example. Our prayer should always be:

1) That others may know Jesus Christ, as their Lord and Savior.

2) That God will keep them from this evil world system, Satan, and all false teaching.

3) That they'll walk in the joy of Jesus Christ.

4) That they'll live Holy lives, including their thoughts, deeds, and character.

5) That they may lead others to Christ and hold on to the faith with the same fervent love that Jesus had.

"Jesus taught them how to pray" *(Luke 11:1-4).*

One of his disciples asked, "Lord teach us to pray." Jesus taught them a model prayer to pray. Jesus knew praying was important.

He breathed on them and sent them out. He didn't show any favoritism even when he knew they were going to deny, betray, and turn their backs on him (Mark 6:7).

As leaders, that's what we should be doing. We should be praying for one another, making other disciples, encouraging each other, and lifting one another up. The strong must bear the infirmity of the weak. James says men should always pray.

The church has to pray without ceasing, but prayer builds your faith in God. Daniel prayed three times a day. When the enemy tried to overtake him, his faith in God remained. He knew God was going to deliver him.

That's how our prayer lives need to be. We need assurance that through our prayers, our righteousness, and our faith in the Lord Jesus Christ, things will change, and circumstances will change. You shouldn't care what this chance looks like because the most important aspect is things will change. The world will change. This world needs a savior; he has already hung, bled, died, and rose again, and he won't do it again. Prayers through the righteous show lives can be changed and saved.

When the righteous call, God will answer. His eyes are on the righteous.

The effective fervent prayer of the righteous availeth much. When we turn our hearts to God and start to earnestly pray, we can see a change in the injustice, prejudice, and lack of love in this world. Jesus has already died and risen again; he's not going to die again. He has given us the power to bind and lose some things.

The only prayer the Lord hears from a non-believer is the prayer of repentance.

We, the believers, have to pray and intercede on behalf of this world, our children, and loved ones. Satan desires to have them and sift them as wheat—hell is real.

Prayer

Father God, you said in your word that the effectual fervent prayer of the righteous availeth much. Holy Spirit, help us, the righteous, to pray without ceasing. Father, you said to call upon you and you will answer and show us great and mighty things we know not of. Lord, we're calling on your Holy and righteous name, hear our prayer and attend unto our prayer.

Father, we come praying for those who are not saved and for those who are saved to have a closer relationship with you. In the name of Jesus Christ, we pray for our co-laborers in the gospel. Holy Spirit, help us to pray for one another and to lift each other up. Help us to have all things common and to encourage each other in the Lord.

Forgive us, Lord, for turning to other things and people, and for not going after you with our whole hearts. You're our deliverer, our healer, and our provider. I pray in the mighty name of Jesus Christ.
Amen.

Wisely Gathering

Day 12

*B*e not deceived: evil communications corrupt good man-ners *(I Corinthians 15:33)*. Why did I hear those words? If it vexes your spirit, it isn't God: no peace, no God. I had an encounter with a couple who vexed my spirit. I started to pray. I heard the Lord say, "Be not deceived: evil communications corrupt good manners." That was my confirmation and my answer to part ways.

Our speech is not the only form of communication. Every part of the body Satan will try to use. "These six things does the Lord hate and; yea, seven are an abomination unto him" *(Proverbs 6:16-19)*.

A proud look signifies arrogance, conceit, self-satisfaction, boasting, and high-mindedness *(Proverbs 6:17, 21:4)*. God wants us to be hum-ble.

When we're prideful, it puts us in direct rebellion against God. We should be clothed with humility; for God resisted the proud, and giveth grace to the humble *(I Peter 5:5c)*. The good news translation states "and all of you must put on the apron of humility, to serve one another." For the scripture says, "God resists the proud, but shows favour to the humble." We must humble ourselves; therefore, under the mighty hand of God, he may exalt you in due time *(I Peter 5:6)*.

A lying tongue represents someone who is not being truthful or telling the truth *(Proverbs 6:17)*. Lying is one of the characteristics of the devil. "Ye are of your father the devil, and the lusts of your father ye will do. He was a murder from the beginning, and abode not in the truth, because there is no truth in him. When he speaketh a lie, he speaketh of his own: for he is a liar, and the father of it" *(John 8:44)*.

God is a God of truth and opposes lying. Jesus says in John 14:6a, "I am the way, the truth, and the life."

Hands that shed innocent blood means murder, or unlawfully taking someone's life *(Proverbs 6:17)*. Thou shalt not kill is the sixth commandment that God gave. A person shall receive the death penalty for violating this commandment. Although we're no longer under the law, in the New Testament, not only does it condemn murder, but also hate and the desire for someone else's death. "But I say unto you, that whosoever is angry with his brother without a cause shall be in danger of the judgment" *(Matthew 5:22a)*.

This is not speaking about a fit of righteous anger for injustice due to hurtful and wicked behavior. This is speaking of malicious and willful intent to harm someone else. He says to the righteous, "Be ye angry, and sin not: let not the sun go down upon your wrath" *(Ephesians 4:26)*. Anger if not controlled will cause a person to want to harm someone else. "Cease from anger and forsake wrath (extreme anger); fret not thyself in any wise to do evil" *(Psalm 37:8)*.

A heart that deviseth wicked imagination implies continuous thoughts of wickedness *(Proverbs 6:18)*. Our heart is the seat of our emotions, and out of the heart are the issues of life *(Proverbs 4:23)*. In Genesis 6:5, it describes the wickedness of man was great, just like the days of Noah, so are the days we are living in. Man is full of wickedness, sexual sins, and violence. The thoughts of a man's heart were continually evil. The Lord made man on the Earth, so it grieved him at his heart *(Genesis 6:5,6)*. Many have pleasure in sin in the sense of taking pleasure in the immoral actions of others, but such sin will be exposed and judged on the day of final judgment *(2 Thessalonians 2:12)*. Paul says in Romans 1:32, they're worthy of death.

Feet that be swift in running to mischief represent someone eager to do wrong or cause harm (Proverbs 6:18). "For as he thinketh in his heart, so is he" *(Proverbs 23:7a)*. If we constantly think about evil, then it's in our hearts. Our feet will follow what's in our hearts. "He that deviseth to do evil shall be called a mischievous person" (Proverbs 24:8). If you're always planning evil, you'll earn a reputation as a troublemaker. Our feet should be shod, or clothed, with the preparation of the gospel of peace (Ephesians 6:15). "How beautiful upon the mountains are the feet of those who bring the happy news of peace and salvation, the news that the God of Israel reign" (Isiah 52:7 TLB)

A false witness who speaks lies signifies the acts of lying, falsifying information, and perjury *(Proverbs 6:19)*. In Matthew 4:6, Satan manipulated, or falsified, the word of God when trying to tempt Jesus to sin. This is the same thing people will do to us. They'll use the scripture out of context to convince or persuade us to do what God dislikes. We, the believers, must know God's word, so we don't fall prey to those who try to distort God's word for their selfish gain.

Timothy tells us to, "Study to shew thyself approved unto God, a workman that needeth not to be ashamed, rightly dividing the word of truth" *(II Timothy 2:15)*. Not what God's word says and means so you're not deceived. The enemy is a false witness to us, and he comes to steal, kill, and destroy *(John 10:10a)*. The enemy will use people who will come to us as false witnesses. They'll speak lies and try to persuade you from the truth.

He that soweth discord among brethren means strife, lack of agreement, not in unity, and variance *(Proverbs 6:19)*. Galatians 5:19-21 gives a list of things controlled by the flesh, one of which is variance, or discord. Paul teaches it's possible to shut oneself out of the kingdom by engaging in evil practices, such as described in Galatians 5:19-21.

When God says to separate, don't mix, just heed to the voice of God. We should be pleasures of God, not man. In Numbers 11:4, the children of Israel had some other folks with them who came from Egypt. They started murmuring, and the children of Israel did the same thing. Evil communication corrupts good manners.

The wrong association can cause you to miss your breakthrough. Everybody can't make the trip, and they can't all function in the same assignment. God sent Moses to deliver the children of Israel from Egyptian bondage.

Prayer

Father God, I bless and praise your holy and wonderful name. Thank you for the gift of the Holy Spirit, who walks alongside me to aid me and help me to make the right decisions. I thank you for giving me an ear to hear and for keeping me. Holy Spirit, help me to guard my ear gates, bridle my tongue, keep my hands from wickedness, and give me a clean heart so I may serve you in spirit and truth. Clothed my feet with the preparation of peace to carry your gospel (the good news of the death, burial, and resurrection) of your darling son Jesus Christ to all of those who are lost. Thank you for your peace and love. In the name of Jesus Christ,

Amen.

You Are Worthy

Day 13

*T*he goodness, greatness, and glory of God. I thought I wasn't worthy of God's goodness, greatness, and glory. I was from a poor family who had all kinds of generational curses. I felt the way Gideon felt: my family was poor, and I was the least in my family *(Judges 6:15)*. God wanted me to see his goodness, greatness, and glory.

God's goodness is given to the just and the unjust.

The glory of God can be seen in his only beloved son, Jesus Christ (Romans 15:7). We don't always deserve God's goodness, but he is such a just and merciful God. We often get what we don't deserve.

David, a man after God's heart *(Psalm 59:1-8)*, committed the unthinkable: adultery, murder. *(2 Samuels 11)*. After he repented with a feeling of Godly sorrow, God showed him his goodness, greatness, and glory.

When Saul was trying to kill David, God's goodness protected him. We have some of Saul in our lives. If we keep our focus on God, he'll show us his goodness and protect us from all of the evil around us.

David saw the Glory of God. After his son tried to kill him, God delivered him and restored all back to him. Even when we think we've lost it all, God will show his glory and restore what the enemy tried to take from us. He tells us in Jeremiah 30:17a, "I will restore health unto thee, and I will heal thee of thy wounds, saith the Lord."

Moses was called to be God's instrument and deliver his people from Egyptian bondage. He says to God, I have a speech impediment. God already knows about our imperfections, yet he still chooses to show the goodness, greatness, and glory of God through us.

God used Moses to deliver the children of Israel. Moses saw the glory of God in the mountains. God is still seeking to give us a mountain-top experience. Saul, who was converted and is called Paul, was saved by God's goodness. He was used by God's greatness to change the world. Christians are still reading and being converted by some of his writings that the Holy Spirit inspired him to write. Paul saw the glory of God. How God used a man who was killing Christians and converted him to be a witness for our Lord and Savior Jesus Christ.

I thought it was too late, but God had a purpose and a plan for my life. Just like the Lord converted Paul, if you're reading this, you can be converted too. It doesn't have to take a Damascus road experience, Acts 9. If you confess your sins, he's faithful and just to forgive us for our sins and to cleanse us from all unrighteousness (I John 1:9). Because of God's goodness and greatness, he'll do what he says he'll do. I'm a living witness; once you see the glory of God, your life will never be the same.

God is awesome. He desires for us to see his goodness, greatness, and glory. I've tried a lot of things, and known of them compared to the goodness, greatness, and glory of God. What did I have to lose? God desires that we see his goodness, greatness, and glory.

Prayer

Father God, I thank you for your goodness, greatness, and glory. If it had not been for you on my side, where would I be? Thank you for being the great I am, and may your glory continue to shine in and through my life. That I may be a candle that never goes out, so men may see my good works that it may glorify you. You're my Redeemer, the lover of my soul. In the name of your darling son Jesus, I pray.

Amen.

Living With Purpose

Day 14

A **virtuous woman is not selfish.** Why was the Lord saying this to me? I was one who would fuss and try to correct my actions by how I thought I should be and act. When I got into the word, I saw what a virtuous woman was and was not. It's not just about being perfect, but all about living life with purpose.

Webster defines virtuous as having or exhibiting virtue (morally good behavior or character).

According to Proverbs 11:16a *(AMP)*, A gracious and good woman attains honor, and we do this by singing praises to God and walking in:

Faith: She'll serve God with all of her heart, mind, and soul. She'll seek his will for her life and follow his ways with fear, or reverent *(Proverbs 31:30)*.

Serving: She'll serve her husband, her family, her friends, and neighbors with a gentle and loving spirit *(Proverbs 31:19-20)*.

Charity: She'll help those in need *(Proverbs 31:20)*. She doesn't grumble while completing her tasks *(Proverbs 31:13, Philippians 2:14)*.

She does not dwell on things that don't please the Lord. Yet, she submits herself unto her husband *(Ephesians 5:22-24)* with love *(Titus 2:4)*, respect *(Ephesians 5:33)*, assistance *(Genesis 2:18)*, and submissiveness *(Ephesian 5:22)* with a gentle and quiet spirit *(I Peter 3:4)*.

Once I received a revelation. I was no longer bothered by what I thought I was supposed to be doing or what my husband was supposed to be doing or not doing. I had to live in obedience as unto the Lord.

The truth of the matter is, while we're pointing fingers and finding faults in others and our mates, we have faults of our own.

I've learned to live a life pleasing the Lord. A woman's highest position of true feminine dignity is as a godly wife and mother; after all, we were created to be a loving companion and helper for our husbands in fulling God's purpose for his life and the life of our family.

As a virtuous woman, "I will praise thee, for I am fearfully and wonderfully made marvelous are thy works; and that my soul knoweth right well" *(Psalm 139:14).*

"I will give thanks and praise to you for I am fearfully and wonderfully made; wonderful are your works, and my soul knows it very well" *(Psalm 139:14 AMP).*

∝

Prayer

Father God, the creator of every good and perfect gift. Forgive me for being judgmental and not appreciating what you have given me. Thank you for opening my eyes to who I am and my purpose. I thank you for the help and guidance of the Holy Spirit who will lead, guide, and teach me how to be and live as the virtuous woman you've called me to be. Help me to be submissive, serving, and loving, as I grow in you and increase my faith. In the name of Jesus Christ, I pray.

Amen.

New Walk

Day 15

*G*o and sin no more, sin stinks in my nostrils. I remembered I had disobeyed God. At the time, I didn't think anything about it. God's timing, though, is not our timing. When he brings it to our remembrance, we should repent and ask for forgiveness. Partial obedience is disobedience.

We've all sinned and fallen short of the glory of God *(Romans 3:23)*.

There's no condemnation for those who are in Christ Jesus, as a result of Jesus' death on the cross. We're forgiven *(Romans 8:1)*.

This does not mean we should keep sinning. We must show the same gratitude that the woman who was caught in the very act of adultery showed. Jesus told her, "Go and sin no more" *(John 8:11)*. That's the same thing he's saying today, "Go and sin no more."

There is a consequence to disobedience, the wages of sin are death, but the gift of God is eternal life. Romans 6:23. We may not die physically but spiritual death is upon us.

Samson's disobedience led him to ruin, but Samson cried out to God one last time, and God answered his prayer. Samson was later listed in the Hebrews chapter of fame. God does not like sin, but it's never too late to turn back to God.

The children of Israel turned their backs on God and went a whoring after strange God's I Chronicles 5:25. The children of Israel, who were God's chosen people, were in bondage for 400 years. They called unto God. God heard their affiliation and used a man by the name of Moses to deliver them from their oppressors. He told Moses, "I heard the cry of my people."

Just like God delivered the children of Israel, Jesus who was born through a virgin, also came to deliver a sin-sick world from sin, sickness, and poverty. His bride is the church (the born-again believers, the call out ones). He said we're in a chosen generation, a royal priesthood. He called us before him and formed us in our mother's womb.

When the children of Israel repented and turned back to God, he delivered them from all their enemies.

God is saying the same thing to us today:

"If my people, which are called by my name (chosen ones, the call out ones) shall humble themselves (humble ourselves before God and confess our sins) and pray (call out to God without ceasing, earnestly pray for God's mercy and forgiveness, trusting he'll hear and answer our prayer), and seek my face (seek God with our whole hearts and his presence); and turn from their wicked ways (genuinely repent and turn from sin and all forms of idolatry, and clean our hands from wickedness and evil) then will I hear from heaven (God will turn away his anger from his people, hear their cries, he'll hear and answer prayers from heaven) and will forgive their sins, and will heal their land (God will begin to pour out his favor and blessings upon his people. God took care of his people (not one feeble-minded person came out of Egypt). Their clothes did not wear out, their feet did not swell."

Christ came to save us, so call on the name of the Lord, our God.

All of these things must be done in the name of our Lord and Savior Jesus Christ *(Colossians 3:17)*. In everything we say, do, or think, it must be done to God's glory, in the name of the Lord, Jesus Christ.

We must turn away from sin. There's no little sin or big sin; sin is sin in the eyes of the Lord.

The world is doing what it wants to do. God is calling for us, the righteous, to pray and live a life as an example to those who are lost.

We've all sinned, but the bible gives us the perfect example by whom we should live by—Jesus Christ, who knew no sin *(I Peter 2:21-25)*. He's the son of God and learned obedience by the things which he suffered *(Hebrews 5:8)*.

We're sons and daughters of God. We cannot cover up sin. If you've fallen, admit your sins, confess, repent. I did, and he forgave me. My daily walk with the Lord is to stay prayerful and constantly ask for forgiveness. Yes, there are times we sin and are not aware of it.

David was the apple of God's eye: he messed up, committed adultery, and murdered a man. When he repented, God forgave him. God is a forgiving God, but there are always consequences to our sins.

David's consequences were "the sword shall never depart from your house" *(2 Samuel 12:10)*. His son raped his daughter, his son killed his son, and then later tried to overthrow him and kill him. Don't let your sins fall onto your children and start generational curses.

We have to lay aside every weight, or sin, that stinks in God's nostrils and is holding us down. We can't let it prevent our prayers from reaching the throne. We must bombard heaven and watch how things turn around. Lives will begin to change; our loved ones will be saved.

Go and sin no more.

Prayer

Father forgive me of my sins. I confess I've sinned against you, and you alone. Forgive me of the sins I'm aware of and those I'm not aware of. Bring them to my remembrance, so I can confess them. You said, if I confess my sins you'll be just and faithful. You'll forgive me and cleanse me from all unrighteousness. Create in me a clean heart and renew a right spirit within me. Father, you made me, and you know all about me. Please cleanse me white as snow and purge me of all of my iniquities. In the name of Jesus Christ, I pray.

Amen.

New Spirit

Day 16

*Y*ou're the church. The church did this to me, and that's why I'm so offended and have the spirit of offense. I was thinking this in my heart, but then I heard, "You're the church."

The offense is annoyance or resentment brought about by a perceived insult to or disregard for oneself or one's standards or principles. it's the action of attacking someone or something.

The spirit of offense will rob you of your blessings. In Mathew 15: 22-28, "the Canaanite woman was called a dog by Jesus."

She came to Jesus saying, "Have mercy on me, O Lord, thou son of David; daughter is grievously vexed with a devil." Jesus ignored her, and the disciples said to send her away.

Jesus answers her and says, "I am not sent but unto the lost sheep of the house of Israel." In this passage, Jesus meant his mission on Earth was confined to the Hebrew nation. He was, as St. Paul calls him, "a Minister of the circumcision" *(Romans 15:8)*. Later, he would send others to evangelize those who were now aliens from the chosen commonwealth; at present, he has come unto his possessions. Lost sheep.

Then, she came and worshipped him, saying, Lord, help me. She worships the Lord.

The purpose of our worship is to glorify, honor, praise, exalt, and please God. The nature of our worship to God demands the prostration of our souls before him in humble and contrite submission. James 4:6 tells us, "God resists the proud, but gives grace to the humble. Humble yourselves in the sight of the Lord, and he will lift you up." Our worship of God is a very humble and reverent action.

Jesus answers her, saying, "it's not meant to take the children's bread and to cast it to dogs."

Bread *signifies the graces and favors bestowed by God in Christ.*

The woman says, "Truth, Lord: yet the dogs eat of the crumbs which fall from their master's table." Jesus answered, "Great is thy faith."

At that time, her daughter is healed. The woman received her blessing. If she had been offended because Jesus called her a dog, her daughter wouldn't have been healed.

How many of us have left our blessings because we're offended?

We should not be caring for the spirit of offense. In Galatians 5:22-23, it says "But the fruit of the Spirit is love, joy, peace, longsuffering, gentleness, goodness, faith, meekness, temperance: against such, there is no law. The spirit of offense is not one of the fruits that Jesus tells us to take on."

So, who is the church?

Every church has issues, which Jesus pointed out in the book of Revelations. He said we lost our first love; so, he tells us to repent. What you're going through is just a test and trial. When the heat of the fire gets hot, he'll refine you.

Once you go through the fire, you'll come through as pure gold; then, go back and do the thing you did when you first fell in love with me.

Nothing you've gone through was for you. Church work does not end. This isn't something new; it's been going on for centuries. Here's what Christ had to say to the seven churches. In Revelation 2-3, he gives exhortation, warning, and edification. The church is not a building. Rather, we, the believers, the body of Christ, is the church).

So, you say the church did this. That's why he left the manual, or bible. He left clear instructions on how we should conduct ourselves. He reveals Satan's tactics used on the church and individual Christians. Always remember Satan's job is to steal, kill, and destroy.

He explains what he loves, hates, the consequences, and the rewards of disobedience.

What's Christ praise? Those who cannot bear those who are evil *(Rev 2:2)*. His message was they don't fall away by tolerating false teachers, prophets, or Apostles, who were distorting his word or weakening its power and authority. He calls them liars.

For the Lord knoweth the way of the righteous; but the way of the ungodly shall perish *(Psalm 1:6)*.

1) The church of **Ephesus** left their first love. They knew correct doctrine, obeyed some commands, and worshipped, but they didn't have a heartfelt love for Christ and his word. They were praised for their hard work and perseverance. He exhorted them to remember, repent, and return. Their reward would be the right to eat from the tree of life.

Modern-day Ephesus, repent and go back to your first love. Some appear as ministers of righteousness, but their teaching contradicts the word of God and leads those following into a spiritual disaster, causing others to be in a backsliding state.

2) The church of **Smyrna** didn't have any warnings. They were praised

for being rich and were exhorted to be faithful. They were poor physically but rich spiritually. They experienced tribulation for 10 days and were encouraged to remain faithful unto death. Their reward would be the crown of life and would not be hurt by the second earth.

Modern-day **Smyrna** be ye steadfast, unmovable, and always abounding in the work of the Lord. Know your labor is not in vain, even though you'll face persecution and abonnement. Your reward is great. He who hath an ear, let him hear what the Spirit has to say. Do not be afraid, do not back down, hold on to the promises of God.

3. The church of **Pergamos** tolerated idolatry and sexual immorality. They were praised for remaining faithful, even unto death. He exhorted them to repent. Their reward would be to eat of the hidden manna, and a white stone with a new name which no man knows except those who receive it.

Modern-day **Pergamos** were opposed by God for their corrupt teaching of Balaam and were leading people into a fatal compromise with immorality worldliness, and false ideologies. They did this for personal advancement and monetary gain. They're to repent, or the Lord will come quickly and fight against them with the sword of his mouth.

The Lord opposes any within his churches who promote a tolerant attitude toward sin. God hates the heresy that teaches we can be saved and, at the same time, live immoral lives. To hate what God hates is an essential characteristic of those loyal to Christ. The fear of the Lord is to hate evil: pride, and arrogancy and the evil way, and the forward mouth, do I hate *(Proverbs 18:13)*.

Those who overcome will eat of the hidden manna and receive a white stone. In the stone, a new name is written, which no man knows.

4) **The church of Thyatira** tolerated idolatry and sexual immorali-

ty. They allowed Jezebel to teach and seduce his servants to commit fornication. They had room to repent and did not. They tolerated sin, unrighteousness, and unbiblical teaching from their leaders. They were praised for their deeds, love and faith, and perseverance. He exhorted them to hold on to what they have until Christ comes. Their reward is the morning star.

Modern-day Thyatira are called Jezebels, these leaders exhibited great charisma with manipulative and seductive influence spirits.

Our own words above Biblical revelation is not acceptable and should not be tolerated, especially because of indifference, personal friendship, fear of confrontation, or because of a desire for peace, harmony, personal advancement, or money.

He says to repent, "I've given you space to repent of fornication, and you have repented not" *(Revelation 2:21)*. God will judge such leaders and punish all those who sin in these ways and do not repent.

5) **The church of Sardis** were not praised. They were criticized for being dead. His exhortation to them was to wake up. Their reward was they would be dressed in white, never blotted out from the book of life.

Modern-day Sardis, the church of Sardis was spiritually dead. They had an outward appearance of being spiritually alive. Jesus saw the absence of the inner reality in their hearts. He saw religion, not spiritual life. They had a form of godliness but denying the power thereof from such turn away.

6) **Church of Philadelphia** were praised for their deeds and faithfulness. They weren't criticized. They were exhorted to hold on to what they had. Their reward would be that they would become a pillar of the temple.

Modern-day **Philadelphia** are those who are faithful to Christ. They kept Christ's word and didn't deny him. They endured opposition and criticism but remained loyal to Christ. God promises to keep the faithful I Philadelphia from the hour of trial. Stay faithful.

7) Church of Laodicea were not praised. They were criticized for being lukewarm. They were neither hot nor cold and were exhorted to be earnest and to repent. They'll be seated with Christ was their reward.

Modern-day **Laodicea** is a lukewarm church that compromises with the world. They're prideful and profess Christ, but they don't know him. Christ invites them to repent and be restored to a place of faith, righteousness, revelation, and fellowship.

Christ is knocking at the door to your heart and wants to come inside. Those who Christ loves, he'll rebuke and chasten them. He that hath an ear, let him hear what the Spirit saith unto the churches.

Only two of the seven churches are not faulted *(Smyrna and Philadelphia)*. Five of the churches, he says, repent. To two of the churches, he says, "Don't be afraid."

Which one are you? Once I read the manual, I was free from "church hurt." I was able to repent and do it all over again.

He that has an ear, let him hear what the spirit has to say.

Prayer

Father God, I bless and praise you for who you are. Thank you, Lord, for showing me myself. Forgive me for carrying the spirit of offense and for offending anyone else. I thank you for your chastisement and for loving me enough to do it. You said those you love you chastise. I honor you, God, for being a loving and compassionate God. Holy Spirit, lead and guide me as I hear what the Spirit has to say. Open my ears to hear on today. In the matchless name of Jesus Christ, I pray.

Amen.

Doing No Harm

Day 17

*T*ouch not my anointed. *The Lord knows our thoughts and what's in our hearts!*

I'd been seeing and hearing some things about pastors. I was thinking in my heart about some of the things and I found myself saying:

What about the Shepherds? After 16 days of breakthroughs and healing, all I could think about was what I had heard and went through. I'm talking about stuff that happened years ago. I wanted the Lord to hurt everybody who had caused me or anybody else any hurt.

After all, the Lord had delivered me and guided me through the breakthroughs I had experienced. So, how could I regress? Well, the enemy comes not but to steal, kill, and destroy. He will try to steal the word from you, kill every promise the Lord has given you, destroy your relationship with the Lord, and destroy your breakthroughs or your deliverance. But Jesus said, "I come that you might have life and have it more abundantly." That's why we have to get into the word. We must know it for ourselves. So, when these thoughts come up, we know how to fight and cast them down. You can only beat Satan with the word. Our battles, oftentimes, start in the mind.

Nothing came out of my mouth; it was in my heart. God knows our inner thoughts and what's in our hearts. Man looks at the outside, but God sees the heart.

The Lord got me straight really fast. He says, "Touch not my anointed and do my prophets no harm" *(I Chronicles 16:22)*. He continues, "and I will give you pastors according to my heart, which shall feed you with knowledge and understanding." *(Jeremiah 3:15)*.

Jesus was a pastor. He taught the people. John, the Baptist, was a preacher. He preached repentance to the people as the forerunner for Jesus Christ He preached, "Repent for the kingdom of heaven is at hand."

Shepherds, also known as pastors, are called to teach, and laymen, also known as preachers, are called to preach *(John 21:15-17)*.

He tells us in Hebrew 13:7, obey them who have the rule over you. Our obedience and faithfulness to our pastors must be based on our loyalty to God. We must love God first *(Matthew 22:37)*, and then to leaders in the church who are loyal to God and his word.

One of the major duties of pastors is to feed the sheep, or flock, by teaching God's word. The flock given to them is the people of God—whom God purchased with the blood of his only begotten son, Jesus Christ. He tells Peter three times to feed his sheep. They're to declare God's whole will by reproving, rebuking, or exhorting with all longsuffering and doctrine *(2 Timothy 4:2)*. They must refuse to seek to please people and say only what they want the people to hear *(2 Timothy 4:3)*.

Remember, the Lord, Jesus, has made them responsible for the lives of all persons under their care *(Acts 20:26-27)*. God will hold them guilty of the blood of all those who are lost because the leader refused to protect the flock from those who weaken and distort the word *(2 Timothy 1:14, Rev. 2:2)*. If any of this applies to you, as it did for me, don't go into details with anyone. Rather, go to the Lord with a sincere heart. Repent, forgive, and move on.

Touch not God's anointed. Put yourself in David's shoes. He had plenty of chances to kill Saul, but he wouldn't touch the Lord's anointed. Even though God had rejected Saul from being the king, he was still God's anointed. David also didn't allow anyone else around him to touch Saul.

God will repay every man for his actions. Respect their office, and let God do the discipline.

Touch not God's anointed, this is not just for the pastors. God gave us— pastors, apostles, prophets, teachers, evangelists, and anyone who is called by God—the same calling, the same rule. I had to repent for my evil thought. If you have these evil thoughts in your mind, repent quickly and let God deal with them.

Prayer

Father God, I know you're an all-knowing, wise, compassionate, and loving God. Please, forgive me for my transgressions. Thank you for loving me so much that you would keep me from falling and keep me on the right path. You are my shield, my provider, and my ever-present help. I cast down every wicked imagination that tries to exalt itself over you. You're the God who can keep me from falling. You said you'll keep me if I keep my mind stayed on you. Holy Spirit, help me to keep my mind on spiritual things. I trust you. I bless you and praise you in the name of Jesus Christ, I pray.
Amen.

Right Path

Day 18

*G*o I have a word for you. This was a challenging day for me. God had been speaking to me very clearly, but I had doubts. Did you say go? That day, I got up super early and started praying. My prayer request was specific, "Lord make a way for me to get out of this. I don't want to go there."

Once I finished praying, the Lord said, "You need to receive an impartation. I have a word for you." I got myself together and went.

The first 45 minutes to an hour was spent praying. I could feel an anointing and God's presence in that room. Every feeling of guilt, unworthiness, and remorse left my body completely. I knew it was God bringing me back, so I could be free and made whole. With the spirit of offense upon me, I wasn't going to be able to effectively do what God has ordained me to do. Thank you, God, for speaking to me. I walked out whole. In addition to being whole, God gave me his word that forever changed my life. "Believe in the Lord thy God, so shall you be established; believe his prophets so shall ye prosper" *(2 Chronicles 20:20c)*. "Don't despise the words from the prophets, after all the Lord did give us prophets; the Lord was with Samuel, and he did not let none of his words fall to the ground" *(I Samuel 3:19)*.

Prophecy: "Woman of God: When you stood, I saw you break completely out of the thing that's been trying to hold you hostage. For me, the spirit of offense was broken that day on September 8th, 2018. Even the sickness that tried to plaque your body today, there's supernatural healing you receive.

I walk in my healing.

The Lord says: don't beat yourself up about anything else. Today forgiveness has been your portion. I'm restoring unto you the years that the cankerworm has eaten, restoration to you today. As a sign, I'll give you beauty for your ashes. There are some things you've been suffering through that you didn't want people to know you've been suffering through. You'd rather suffer in silence before you let people know how vulnerable and how broken you were. The Lord said he is a repairer of the breach. Your bridge is reconstructing itself, and he's given you the ability to cross over. You will not go through another season feeling like you are by yourself, or empty and feeling alone.

He has given you a family who loves and supports you and will cover you.

You have too much anointing in your belly and the enemy has tried to plague you. Not only will the Lord give you a breakthrough, but your daughter who is suicidal (after that statement everything else was vague. Only God could tell him something like that, he didn't know anything about what my daughter was going through). The remainder of the prophecy I only have fragments of. He was going to deliver me from the woods (and he described the area in which I live, and he had never been there). I will count more money than I ever counted in my life.

I thought day three was the day, but day three only helped me to get through the storm that was heading my way.

I did not get the revelation of, "The Lord said, he's a repairer of the breach; your bridge is reconstructing itself and he's given you the ability to cross over," until August 19th, 2020. I was sitting and just kept hearing, "repairing the breach." I heard it over and over. I thought to myself, *where do I know that phrase from?* I heard the Holy Spirit say "prophecy." I went to my manuscript and there it was, sitting in the middle of day 18.

A repairer is a skilled worker who mends or repairs things.

A breach is a gap in a wall, barrier, or defense, especially one made by an attacking army. A bridge is constructed to reconcile or form a connection between two things. Reconstructing is to build or form again after it has been damaged or destroyed.

God is the repairer of the breach. There was a breach in my relationship with God. God had told me to leave Louisiana and move to Mississippi. There was an anointing that needed to be imparted into me. Satan had attacked my mind and

...t I had to believe in God and my spiritual leaders.

God repaired the breach in our relationship. Now my bridge with God has been repaired by my confessions and all his forgiveness.

When there is a true love for God, a channel is opened for God's full blessing to come into our lives. The rewards for such love are:

1) The light of God and the full joy of salvation and healing.

2) God's protection and presence manifested in our lives.

3) God's help in trouble through answered prayers.

4) The lifting of darkness and oppression.

5) God's guidance, strength, and fruitfulness.

6) True restoration.

For those of you who don't believe in prophets, the word of God is a sure word of prophecy. God still has prophets in the Earth realm.

Beware of false prophets, get in the word, and ask God for the spirit of discernment. This way you'll be able to discern if a prophecy is from God.

Prayer

Father God, I thank you with a sincere heart for opening the eyes of my understanding. Thank you for repairing and reconstructing the breach that only you can do. You said in your word to draw nigh unto you and you will draw nigh unto me. Holy Spirit, help me to hold on to the promises of God. You're my helper, lead, and guide. You'll make sure I stay on the path God has for me. I thank you now, Lord, for restoring my relationships. You've proven to be my shield and my exceedingly great reward. It's in the matchless name of Jesus Christ, I pray.

Amen.

Prayer Focus

Day 19

*S*elfish prayer: Why did I hear that? I'd been praying and praying about something for myself. I was praying for myself when I should've been praying for others.

One of my favorite prayers is the prayer of Jabez. When I first started praying that prayer, "Oh that you would bless me indeed," it was for material things and selfishness *(I Chronicles 4:9-10)*.

As I studied the life of Jabez, he was not a forerunner in the scripture for his incredible talents or gifts. Nothing is mentioned about how he contributed or what he accomplished. In I Chronicles 4:9, God points out he was more honorable than his brothers. This is very encouraging because honor and integrity are qualities any of us can strive to achieve. When we do, God is much more inclined to hear and answer our prayers, just as he did for Jabez.

God considered Jabez "honorable," and then he included his prayer in the bible. God considered this a remarkable example for us to follow. We don't need to know about his life before this prayer. Romans 15:4 tells us, "for whatsoever things were written aforetime were written for our learning, that we through patience and comfort of the scriptures might have hope."

One commentary explained this verse like this: The more we know about what God has done in years past, the greater the confidence we have about what he'll do in the days ahead. That's why it's important to read our bibles diligently to increase our trust that God's will is best for us.

The prayer Jabez prayed starts off by saying, **"And Jabez called on the God of Israel"** *(I Chronicles 4:10a)*. He started it off perfectly by calling upon the God of Israel. In Jeremiah 33:3, the Lord tells us, "Call unto me and I will answer thee, and shew thee great and mighty things, which though knowest not." "Call to me, and I will answer you; I will tell you wonderful and marvelous things that you know nothing about" *(GNB)*.

Now do you see why Jabez's prayer was answered? He was honorable, and he called upon the Lord God of Israel, the only God who hears and answers prayers.

Now when I pray this prayer, it's not for my selfishness. It's for spiritual things: a closer walk with the Lord and for others, especially those who are hurting or in need.

"Oh, that thou wouldest bless me indeed" *(I Chronicles 4:10b)*.

Bless me to be a blessing. Jabez was asking God to bless him a lot. This is not selfish at all, but we must have the right motives. In Exodus 34:6, God proclaimed he was merciful, gracious, longsuffering, and abundant in goodness and truth. Are you convinced? If not, Psalm 34:10 tells us, "The young lions do lack, and suffer hunger: **but they that seek the Lord shall not want any good thing.**" In Psalm 86:5, it says, "For though, Lord art good, and ready to forgive; and plenteous in mercy unto all them that call upon thee."

In Mathew 7:7-8, Jesus says: ask and it'll be given to you; seek and you'll find; knock and it'll be opened to you. Everyone who asks receives what they want. Everyone who seeks finds what they need. Everyone who knocks gets doors opened.

And enlarge my coast *(I Chronicles 4:10c)*.

> Enlarge my anointing and enlarge my relationship with God. Increase me with wisdom and knowledge.
>
> Enlarge my love walk and increase my faith.
>
> Give me a greater infilling of the Holy Spirit and increase my prayer life.

Increase my giving (if he increases your giving, he'll increase your income) and that thine hand might be with me.

Give me your anointing that destroys yolks and lifts burdens and that thine wouldest keep me from evil *(I Chronicles 4:10d).*

We need the Holy Spirit upon us to keep us from evil. What happens a lot of times is that once God blesses us, we start worshipping and praising the creation more than the creator.

When obedience kicks in and God starts giving us more, increasing our ministry (whatever it is God calls us to do), then our adversary starts attacking us. As long as we're not concerned about our spiritual growth, the devil is not worried about us. He knows we're not doing anything.

Once we start stepping out and walking in faith, the enemy will come and attack us. The enemy will start in our minds. We need the Lord to keep us from evil. We cannot live an abundant life and enjoy God's blessings if evil is present.

Jabez asked God **to keep him from evil**. In the society we live in today, we need God to keep us from evil. Jabez was asking God to not even let him approach that which will tempt him to sin. In Job 1:8, it declared that Job eschewed evil and feared God.

"Eschewed means to avoid something intentionally, fear in this text means to reverence, have deep respect."

In Luke 22:40, Jesus told his disciples to "pray that you may not enter into temptation." We have to pray that we enter not into temptation.

That it may not grieve me *(I Chronicles 4:10e).*

Jabez needed God to keep him from evil so it may not grieve him or cause him distress or pain. When we sin, it'll cause us pain. The wages of sin are death, but the gift of God is eternal life *(Romans 6:23).*

When we sin, our spiritual relationship with God dies. We have to always be alert to the enemy's tricks and schemes. And we must resist temptation. We have a greater one working on the inside of us. "Greater is he who is in you than he who is in the world" *(John 4:4)*. God has the power to protect us.

And God granted him that which he requested *(I Chronicles 4:10f)*.

God is an awesome God. He's delighted to see his children blessed. We're his children. The blessings of the Lord will maketh rich and addeth no sorrow with it *(Proverbs 10:22)*. "It is the Lord's blessing that makes you wealthy. Hard work can make you no richer" *(GNB)*.

Unanswered prayers can be difficult and painful, but you must continue to pray. Pray for healing. Pray for our leaders. Pray for our future generation. Pray in unity with the Holy Spirit. Sometimes, we might not know what to pray for. "Likewise, the Spirit also helpeth our infirmities: for we know not what we should pray for as we ought: but the Spirit itself maketh intercession for us with groanings which cannot be uttered. And he *(Holy Spirit)* that searcheth the hearts knoweth what is the mind of the Spirit because he maketh intercession for the saints according to the will of God" *(Romans 8:26-27)*.

God told Moses to rehearse it in Joshua's ears because he became a great leader. I know Moses was praying for Joshua. When Josue became the leader after Moses died, he told Israel to rehearse it in the ears of their children.

James put's it like this, "The effectual fervent prayer of a righteous man availeth much" *(James5:16b)*.

Prayers change things. Elisha was a man with passion like you and me, and he prayed it wouldn't rain, and it did not rain for 3 ½ years *(James 5:17; I Kings 17:1)*.

God hears and answers the prayers of the righteous, but we have to pray the prayer of faith and make sure we're not praying selfish prayers. We should be praying in line with God's will, not our own will.

Prayer

Father God, I come before our throne asking you to forgive me for my selfishness and forgive me for thinking about myself. Father, I humbly come praying for my brothers and sisters in Christ, in the name of Jesus Christ. Holy Spirit, help us to pray. We don't know what to ask for, but you know all things. Please help us to pray in harmony with you. Take our petitions with groanings and mourning unto the Lord, search our hearts, and give us ears to hear what the spirit has to say. In the name of Jesus Christ, I pray.

Amen.

Prove Your Faith

Day 20

*I*t's just a test. But through your test, I'll raise you up. God does test our faith. Abraham was 100 years old when Isaac was born. The Lord told him to offer him up as a sacrifice. Abraham obeyed.

I've come to realize that some of the things I went through were just a test of my faith and others were just my disobedience. Disobedience will cause you to be in the belly of a whale, or a place not ordained by God. The only way out is for God to cause that whale, or anything that has swallowed you up, to spew you out of his belly. Be obedient to what God is telling you to do, no matter how you feel.

Stay in faith, even when the enemy wants to get you out of faith. In I Peter 1:6,7, the living bible paraphrased the passage: "So be truly glad! There is wonderful joy ahead, even though the going is rough for a while down here. These trials are only to test your faith, to see whether or not it is strong and pure. It is being tested as fire tests gold and purifies it—and your faith is far more precious to God than mere gold; so, if your faith remains strong after being tried in the test tube of fiery trials, it will bring you much praise and glory and honor on the day of his return."

In Luke 22:31-32a, Jesus tells Simoon (Peter) that Satan hath desired to have him, that he may sift him as wheat, but I have prayed for thee, that thy faith fail not.

Just like Jesus prayed for Peter, our Lord and Savior Jesus Christ is sitting at the right hand of the father making intercessions on our behalf *(Hebrews 7:25)*.

The enemy can't win when you stay in faith. Hebrews 11:1 gives us a description of faith, but the definition of faith is total trust and reliance upon God. We must:

1) Seek God.

2) Believe in his goodness.

3) Have confidence in his word.

4) Obey his commands.

5) Regulate our life on his promises.

6) Reject the Spirit of this present world.

7) Refuse the pleasure of sin.

8) Endure persecution.

9) Suffer for God.

When we stand in faith while going through these trials, our faith and trust in God will increase.

Hebrews 11:2 tells us, "For by it (faith) the elders obtained a good report. Our patriarchs left examples for us; each one demonstrates a different aspect of a life in faith" *(Hebrews 11:4-13)*.

(1) Abel—by faith, he offered a more excellent sacrifice than Cain to God. He was a righteous man. This is a form of worship, and Abel worshipped God with his giving *(Hebrews 11:4)*.

(2) Enoch—he walked with God and didn't see death. He pleased God. During the times of Enoch, they were wicked, but he refused the pleasure of the world and walked with God *(Hebrews 11:5)*.

(3) Noah—he was warned by God of the things to come. By faith, he believed in God, and he and his family were spared. He became the heir of righteousness by faith. God spoke to Noah and he listened to God. Even though the word poked and made fun of him, he chose to listen to God *(Hebrews 11:7)*.

(4) Abraham—by faith, he obeyed God. He was called to go to a place he didn't know. Faith and obedience go hand-in-hand. Abraham obeyed the command of God. He promised he'd be the father of many nations *(Hebrews 11:8-10)*.

(5) Sara—she conceived and had a child past childbearing age. She judged God faithful because he promised (Hebrews 11:1).

Have faith and trust in God. Faithfulness to God does not guarantee comfort or deliverance from persecution in this world. But it does assure us of God's grace, help, and strength in times of persecution, trials, or suffering. The just shall live by his faith *(Habakkuk 2:4b)*. **It's just a test of your faith.**

Prayer

Father God, I come before you, asking to increase my faith the more. You said without faith it's impossible to please God. You've given us all a measure of faith and some the gift of faith. Holy Spirit, help me not to lean unto my own understanding but to acknowledge you, God, in all ways, so you can direct my path. Keep me, Lord, on the path you've designed for me. So, when my faith is tried and tested, I won't be moved but will look to the hills from to where my help comes from, all of my help comes from you, Lord.

Father, I bless your holy name. Only you're able to keep me. In the name of Jesus Christ, I pray.
Amen.

Change Is Coming

Day 21

*I*t's a new day. Behold, I'll do a new thing, now it shall spring forth; shall ye not know it? I'll even make a way in the wilderness, and rivers in the desert *(Isaiah 43:19)*.

It was prophesied to me that God was going to deliver me out of the wilderness. Today, I was seeing myself out of the wilderness. I heard, "It's a new day."

I know God will do what he said because God is not a man who would lie, neither the son of man, that he should repent; hath he said, and shall he not do it? Or hath he spoken and shall he not make it good. Everything the Lord has told me he was going to do has come to pass thus far. There are still some things he has promised me that I'm waiting on, but and I know it shall come to pass. "But they that wait upon the Lord shall renew their strength; they shall mount up with wings as eagles; they shall run, and not be weary; and they shall walk, and not faint" *(Isaiah 40:31)*. "Wait on the Lord; be of good courage, and he shall strengthen thing heart; wait, I say, on the Lord" *(Psalm 27:14)*. It's a new day and a new strength. I shall wait upon the Lord.

It's a new day for me. You must see yourself where God has promised to take you or do for you. I encourage you to "Lift up your heads, O ye gates; and be ye lift up, ye everlasting doors; and the King of glory shall come in. Who is this King of glory? The Lord strong and mighty, the Lord mighty in battle" *(Psalms 24:7,8)*.

If you're still feeling frustrated or doubtful, ask yourself if it's because you're not walking in your purpose?

The Lord told Moses to speak to the rock, and Moses struck the rock. Moses was not walking in his purpose. He became frustrated with the people when they started murmuring and complaining.

Moses' purpose was to lead the people following God's instructions. The only thing he had to do was follow God's instructions and do what God said for him to do. That's why we're frustrated. We're doing things out of our strength and not listening to the voice of God. We must listen. "He that has ears let him hear what the Spirit has to say" *(Revelation 2:7)*. Even if we don't like it, we have to do what the Lord has called us to do. Moses' disobedience caused him not to go to the promise land. What is yours causing you?

For I know the thoughts that I think toward you, said the Lord, thoughts of peace, and not of evil, to give you an expected end *(Jeremiah 29:11)*.

The Lord is the only one who can help you fight this battle, regardless of what the battle is. Always remember to walk in your purpose.

This is a new day; one the Lord has made. Get up, pray, and hear the voice of God. See what the Lord has to say to you. He is speaking.

⤚⤙

Prayer

Hallelujah, Praise the Lord. This is a day the Lord has made, and I'll rejoice and be glad in it. Father God, I thank you for this day, one I've never seen before and one I'll never see again. Thank you, Father, for new beginnings. It's in you I live, I move, and I have my being. Thank you, Lord, for new opportunities. Stir up every gift that is on the inside of me. Father, I praise you and bless your Holy name. You didn't have to do it, but you did. I lift up my voice like a trumpet in Zion and give you the praises that are due to your name. I thank you for your strength and victory in winning this war. Holy Spirit, help me to walk in purpose and on purpose. Father, I know you have a plan and it's a good plan for my life. I love you and honor you, Lord. I'm forever grateful for this new day and new blessings. In the matchless name of Jesus Christ, I pray.

Amen.

I hope you were blessed with this 21-day walk with the Lord. Surely his voice has blessed me and forever changed my life. Know who you are in the Lord and follow the manual that has already been written *(The Word of God)*. "Not by might nor by power, but by my Spirit," says the Lord almighty *(Zechariah 4:6 NIV)*.

The Lord is doing a new thing in me. Eyes have not seen, nor ears heard…

Unless otherwise indicated, Scripture quotations are taken from the King James version of the Bible, amplified bible, GNB, the message bible, Life in the Spirit, The Living Bible.

Foreword

*T*he word of God admonishes his people to lean on him and allow him to begin and continue the process of healing your brokenness. One of God's promises is "He heals the brokenhearted and binds up their wounds (curing their pains and their sorrows)" *(Psalm 147:3 AMP)*.

The King James verse states God healeth the broken in heart, which means a continuation of God's healing power. He cures your wounds, scars, and brokenness, and restores your total life to wholeness.

God gives us an invitation to come to the Spiritual Physician who never fails to heal. A broken heart can be in the form of physical, emotional, or spiritual. But God, who is our great physician, can do divine surgery and bring wholeness to your inner being.

Elder Tawana has been transparent in exposing her broken wounded soul and uncovering the hidden darkness of life's harsh reality. She reveals and discusses taboo subjects that are often concealed.

Healing is a process that takes courage, faith, and reliance on God our father.

This 21-day journey will inspire, enlighten, and awaken your spirit to allow God to take you from "brokenness to wholeness."

Dr. Eunice W. Rush, Senior Pastor and Founder of Faith, Hope and Deliverance Ministries, Wiggins, Mississippi.

Dean of Shekinah Glory College of Christian Training.

God says, "I will restore health to you, and I will heal your wounds because people have called you an outcast and (a broken vessel which cannot be healed) whom no one seeks after and for whom no one cares" (Jeremiah 30:17). Amplified. But God is our healer.

Dr. Eunice W. Rush

About the Author

Tawana Conner

*S*he is an Elder at Faith, Hope and Deliverance Ministries, 48 Shadeville Road, Wiggins, Ms. Dr. Eunice, and Apostle Eric Rush, Pastors. She was born and raised in Norco, La., educated in the St. Charles Parish School system. The daughter of Joseph Lee and Ada Mae Harding, the wife of Tommie Lee Conner, and have five beautiful children. A board member of RG MindfulHealth 4 Our Youth (a nonprofit organization) in Gulfport, MS. She loves the Lord and has a passion for ministry. She's a professional leader at People's Health Network a Medicare Advantage Plan in Metairie, LA for over 20 years. Elder Tawana's passion is ministering to hurting women, especially those who have experienced domestic, physical, mental, and/or verbal abuse.

Notes to myself

www.ingramcontent.com/pod-product-compliance
Lightning Source LLC
Chambersburg PA
CBHW021954090426
42811CB00001B/27